GROWING UP, GROWING DOWN

The Story of A Nearly Man

Copyright © 2025 **Jonathan Wright**

All rights reserved. No part of this publication may be reproduced, distributed, or transmitted in any form or by any means without the prior written permission of the author.

Dedication

This book is dedicated to my beloved departed mother, Winifred May Wright nee Olivier.

About the Author and his book

This book is written by Johnny Wright, who, on publication, will be 83, possibly the oldest first-time author in the UK, overtaking Mary Wesley, whose first book – "Jumping the Queue"- was published in 1983. She was 71. Wright's book is fictional, although a certain amount of the content is admittedly autobiographical.

Mr. Wright is currently engaged in writing a series of books, "Where are they now?" – all concerned with the latter days of famous fictional characters such as "Biggles" and "Bunter".

"GROWING UP and GROWING DOWN"

The Life of Julian Bright, a Nearly Man

This is the story of the life and times of Julian Bright, from his birth in World War 2 to today when he is an ailing eighty-year-old.

His widowed Mother brought up five sons, the youngest of whom is Julian, who never knew his father.

We see him through schools in the private sector, where one of his grandparents, Allen Olivier, his Mother's father, generously supports him financially. He does quite well at his schools both academically and physically but not very well. We see early signs of his being a 'nearly man' across the board. His family feels that he should not go to University but get a job.

He joins Metal Box, a large can-making company, where he does well on the Production Control side. He has moved around the country and gained early promotions mostly by working hard and well.

He wants to move into Marketing, cooler and better paid.

He moves to Chesebrough-Pond's, an American Toiletry and Cosmetic company, and makes the hoped-for move into Marketing with the new company's Irish office. He then is promoted back to London, and then after a couple of near misses for further promotions, he makes another, much-wanted move into Advertising, even cooler with certainly more money, and there are other attractions, including a car.

Throughout his life and this story, Julian is obsessed with girls. He has many relationships, work, sports, and church-related.

Both sides of his family are associated with and influenced by The Plymouth Brethren. But, the unacceptable behaviour of the PB leadership led to a major schism in the sect, and the entire Bright Family left for a more orthodox practice of Christianity.

Julian, now an experienced adman, founded Bright and Partners with some friends, but apart from a certain amount of kudos for being the first Agency to act for the Labour Party, Bright and Partners is not a success, and Julian goes out on his own as an advertising Consultant specialising in teaching Best Practices all over the world, earning a great deal of money and travelling a huge number of miles.

His long marriage breaks up largely due to his frequent absences, and it seems that a contributing factor may possibly be the arrival of Alzheimer's.

He maintains a sort of drifting contact with his ex-wife and his three grown-up daughters.

But the long-term prognosis is not good. We leave him as he is drifting towards an uncertain future after a nearly satisfactory life.

Table of Contents

Acknowledgement .... Error! Bookmark not defined.

Dedication i

About The Author and his book ii

Chapter 1. Being a Boy- a start togrowing up. 1

Chapter 2. Being a Son-low on the family pecking-order,high on sex 8

Chapter 3. Becoming a Man,mostly in a Happy Family 14

Chapter 4. Being a Brother of the Plymouth persuasion 18

Chapter 5. Being in fresh woods and pastures new 25

Chapter 6. Becoming a worker- cans, cosmetics, commercials, skittles and netball 28

Chapter 7. Being in Ireland loving my flat,my job, the girls and the Guinness but not being Irish 34

Chapter 8. Being back in London, capital of the Ad world and Champion of laughter at work. 38

Chapter 9. Beginning to become a bona fide Madman-a real player in an unreal world, girls, ads, cash, and the black stuff. 41

Chapter 10. Being Bright and beautiful- name over the door …..briefly! 43

Chapter 11. Becoming a traveller- around the days in eighty worlds 47

Chapter 12 The benefits of being around great men 50

Chapter 13. Being in tune humming the good, the bad and the ugly. 54

Chapter 14. Being a friend 56

Chapter 15. Being at a loss 58

Chapter 16. Beginning to become ill – a start to growing down. 59

Chapter 17. Being a Father and meeting the Demented Ant 62

Chapter 18. Unbecoming or unravelling 66

Chapter 19. Nearly done after nearly doing nearly everything 69

Chapter 1.

Being a Boy

The dramas of JB's early years – his father's death, the War, his much loved and influential grandfather's house being bombed, and the Family's precious collection of shrapnel was 'taken off our hands.' He was born at home in Redhill in June 1942, roughly halfway through the Second World War. His father, Edmund, died of septicaemia in February 1943, never to enter my consciousness, so he had no recollection of him or anything about him but leaving his Mother, Olive, a widow at thirty-four with five sons aged from the oldest, Edmund Junior at eleven to me at nearly one. Having gone to Oxford to read the curiously named 'Greats,' his father had made the equally curious career move to join his father's accountancy firm, in the certain knowledge that he would be bored stiff for all his working life. Something his Mother much later confirmed to be as fully achieved as he had feared. He was, his Mother once told me – "Edmund was a better father than a husband"-but it is difficult to understand quite what this means. Is it a good or a bad thing?

Once, some years later, His father's early death obviously left a substantial void, which Julian never fully acknowledged but which was swiftly filled by the mighty character, his Mother, who, without batting an eye-lid, indeed any sort of lid, ran a large happyish family pretty well with a constant smile on her cheeks until Julian and his brothers had left school some eighteen years later. The family, as such, began to go their separate ways. She never married again- well, who would take on an all-male, costly group of five pushy lads, not one of whom had yet started to earn, led by a very strong-minded matriarch who tended to relish her leadership role and who liked to carry on demonstrating her love for the sport, and her undoubtedly superior sporting skills on a continuing basis for many years? In addition to sports, she also loved music, playing the piano, and singing both lustily and accurately. She also seemingly loved her children and, when they arrived, her grandchildren, whom she adored, possibly more than the children, an endless stream of dogs (mostly cocker-spaniels) and cats (mostly strays).

A special part of my Mother's life was her religion. Her parents and, as a matter of fact, my father's parents were active members of a strict evangelical Protestant order called the Plymouth Brethren. This was a major factor in both his Mother's and father's lives, but in due course, it was much less influential for the five brothers. It was my Mother's belief that this "helped make us such nice people." Events of later years might call this into question!

The second family war-time drama, again a little too early for me to remember it personally, was the arrival of a German incendiary bomb in the corner of our neighbour's garden, a corner we shared. In itself, not necessarily too alarming, but unknown to us, this particular corner housed our friend's entirely illicit and well-camouflaged store of petrol. The ensuing conflagration was hugely dramatic. The more so because our side of this corner was where our Mother had arranged for a very necessarily and totally legal chicken-run to be built. Not only did the chicken-house disappear in an instant, but all ten chickens, with no particular place to go, caught fire and took to the air, Flying Barbecues as they were immediately called – a newly invented British incendiary device. One of our brothers, Edmund Junior, moved swiftly, nimbly plucking two of the FBs from the air while Tim, my tallest brother, was, like a basket-ball player, able to pluck another FB from the branches of a tree, and our Mother served them as roast chicken that evening, a rare war-time meat dinner. My Mother, in return for appropriately keeping mum about the matter, successfully negotiated with an embarrassed but guilty neighbour for equally suitable compensation- a new run and a new flock of live chickens and, less appropriately, a case of sherry.

The next piece of family wartime drama occurred in June 1944 when my grandfather's Croydon house, about two miles from our house, was struck full on by a German V2 bomb, a doodle-bug, which sliced off the entire front of the house like the proverbial knife going through butter, passing some three feet from my grand-father lying in his mighty bed in which he insisted on staying and usually sleeping tolerably well ignoring come whatever the German Luftwaffe might throw at or drop on him. My grandmother meanwhile, their two younger daughters- Aunts Joy and Rachel- and the staff: the Bunkers- Alf, Maud, and Martha and the Acock families- Nanny Beatrice and her younger sister, Nanny Annie, both looking exactly like each other, pleasantly ugly, Quentin

Blake look-alikes, cowered nightly in the cellar or in the Anderson Shelter trying to sleep on camp-beds and, from now on, extensively open to the air encircled by rubble. Open too to circling looters, adept, it transpired, at retrieving Auntie Rachel's hand-bag and sundry knick-knacks.

Nanny Beatrice had one extraordinary and macabre skill. She was probably the best wasp-killer of her time. Armed with a pair of scissors, she was able to cut wasps in half in flight- an unusual and valued capability.

The exciting parts of the War in 1945 were split in two. In the Spring, my fourth brother, James, not only caught measles, appropriately of the German variety, but he made very sure that my other three brothers- firstly, my eldest brother, Edmund Junior, then Michael and Tim- all became Germanically infected albeit briefly while I, by now three, avoided catching it altogether. One of these powerful early memories was that of my brother, James, suffering from measles, lying blubbing rather pathetically on a camp bed in the part of the cellar that served us as our sick room. His mocking brothers' total lack of sympathy failed to help restore his health or his morale. In fact, there was a fraternal tendency to giggle.

I was subsequently told that although I may have escaped it, of the sixty or so younger children living on our street, everyone caught it, bar me. My Mother and I, both virus free, were held, totally unfairly, to be entirely to blame throughout the neighbourhood for both its arrival and its spread. Perhaps curiously, illness avoidance remained one of my strengths for much of my life until many years later, when I succumbed to Covid fashionably but not terminally.

The War ended on 2nd September 1945. However, my War finished a couple of weeks earlier when a big Victorian house about two miles from us and around two hundred yards from our grandfather's frontless house was hit by two, possibly three, of the last V2 bombs of the War. In line with one of the normal youthful actions of the War, for the last time, as it so happened, all five brothers, Julian in a pram, went to inspect the site and to retrieve any shrapnel that might be lying about the carcass of the house. It was a wondrous haul, possibly world-beating, five big, blue Milo tins absolutely full and absolutely pointless loaded around me in my pram. This shrapnel mountain, a mighty edifice of very limited value and of zero beauty, much hated by my Mother (not the most orderly or tidy of house-holders), remained an ugly central feature of wherever our Mother lived until my eldest brother, Edmund Junior, (who, as the oldest, laid an undeniable claim to ownership of the shrapnel cache) got married some ten years later. Our Mother suggested that while the newly-weds were honey-mooning in Devon, there would be an opportunity for the rest of us to clear away the shrapnel - there was, she said, a scrap-metal merchant in West Croydon, who, she thought, might buy our shrapnel trove as scrap. She was right in every respect except for the important one of 'buying,' which he nearly did, but he was more inclined 'to take it off our hands,' which he preferred, and then duly did just that. All our shrapnel had gone to a new home- a fact for which we, the four remaining brothers, were never forgiven by our eldest brother, although Margaret, his new wife, seemed more inclined to live happily ever after without the shrapnel pile. Edmund believed this to be interfamilial theft, actively considered reporting this serious matter to the police, and talked of it as such for the rest of his life not only to us, his family, to Margaret, in due course to their children and, further down the track but not much, to Jenny, his second wife, whose total lack of interest in shrapnel did not perhaps help get the marriage off to the best of starts but swiftly replaced as lead interest by two children, our first nephew and niece, who seemed rather curiously to be roughly my age.

The end of the War led immediately to the beginning of my education. My Mother, faced with the need to find a suitable school for her youngest son, who was now approaching four years old, speedily found several options, all much of a muchness, but she favoured a nearby Dame school- Miss Doubleton's- where Julian went in September 1946, when he turned four, and which turned out to be entirely satisfactory. A welcome turn of events was that the small school had a very large, beautifully kept lawn used every day in the main for PT and in the summer for cricket. It also had just two lady teachers, Miss Johnson and Miss Doubleton herself, both of whom were besotted by cricket as, coincidentally, was our Mother, by a distance, the best bowler in the family. Coming from a family of boys, it would have been impossible to imagine that the entire family, the Brights, would not be anything but similarly besotted. Julian, it turned out, was the best player, he kindly told us, originally a sort of all-rounder but latterly a specialist bowler, was also nearly very good at it because as well as frequent school cricket, we had family cricket on our own lawn at home dominated by my medium-paced Mother almost every day and in 1947 it was a memorably hot, dry summer and rainless autumn so the Misses Doubleton and Johnson encouraged cricket almost every morning. On his first morning, aged five, he scored 37, a score which he never approached again until I made 91 when 15 at his 'big' school, and he scored three other scores in the 90s, but never 100- he was so very much a nearly man in most aspects of his life-. Miss Johnson taught Maths, Geography, and PE, and Miss Doubleton taught English, History, and Scripture. He loved this school although it would not have been manly to say so - so he didn't – and, anyhow, it was the cricket, first and foremost, that he loved. He stayed there until he was seven when he went, as one did in those days, to a Prep School - The Cedars - which only took boarders, so all the Brights went as weekly boarders. Although, like many of the other boys away from home for the first time, Julian suffered a bit from homesickness, but overall, he enjoyed it and did quite well there in most subjects, except for Maths (too difficult) and Geography (too dull), and in all sports but especially cricket. He stayed for six years, and he thought he was probably going to be, firstly, House Captain and then possibly Head Boy. He reckoned he nearly got to be both, but in fact, he failed to be appointed to either post, finishing, he chose to think, as runner-up both times. He left The Cedars after taking the Common Entrance Examination when he was thirteen. I also took the Scholarship exam for St. Jude's, a local public school, which, if I had passed, would have meant free education. I did quite well but not well enough.

The school took me in and did, in the end, grant my Mother a 50% reduction of the fees- a worthwhile and generous saving but, unfortunately, not nearly enough. My Mother simply could not afford the fees. However, our grandfather, her father, Allen Olivier, stepped in and generously agreed to pay the rest. One of her two brothers, William, a doctor, was similarly naturally generous with monthly payments until all five brothers left school when each of us was eighteen. Her second brother, Keith, quite a good earner as a senior manager in the family timber firm, contributed nothing, a natural meanie. When it was time for Julian to leave school, our Mother and the whole family all sat down to tea and gave very serious thought to what I was going to do next and how it was going to be funded. Money was one of the key reasons, but not the only one, why Julian did not go to University. Instead, he looked for and got an earning job.

When he looked back at his years at St Jude's, he had very mixed feelings. He did not start very well. His first form master, Kenneth Ball, was a bully, a man of size but with no charm and very little intelligence. In his first year-end report, he accused Julian of bullying in writing. Our Mother, a feisty lady, was horrified by this entry in the School Report and challenged it. Ball said her son had on two occasions been reported to him for fighting two younger boys- Graham Carrier and Michael Hewitt, and he had, in fact, been beaten by Ball himself for these offenses at the time. My Mother knew the carriers and went to see Mrs. Carrier possibly to apologise. Graham Carrier was about my age, much bigger (fatter!) than me, and agreed we had had a scuffle but denied that he had ever been bullied him or bullied Julian in return. He said we were friends, and, as a matter of fact, we still are. Michael Hewitt, younger than me and in a lower form, was already on the way to becoming a very good rugby player and demonstrably tougher than me. My Mother arranged to meet his father, who just dismissed the whole affair and instructed Mr. Ball to remove the "charge" from my report, which he reluctantly did.

After that opener, I did pretty well but not very well. I was nearly a star but not quite - the story of my life.

Academically, I was alright. I took and passed six" O-Levels" in 1958, only six because I took them all a year earlier than usual when he was sixteen and was regarded as well above average bright, then two years later I passed two "A-Levels" English and History. Nowadays, I would have got A* grades on both, but that grading had not been introduced by then.

I stayed on into the Upper Sixth, a final year doing not a lot. It was while I was not doing that lot that one of the masters- Paul Scott - a Geography teacher, found me and others fooling around in a changing room after cricket. He admonished me not so much for the actual foolery but because it was I, "perhaps the brightest boy in the school," who was doing the fooling.

Again, I had thought at one stage I might be Head Prefect, and quite nearly was, but in the end, this was not to be. I thought I might be House Captain, and this time I was but probably should not have been - his bosom pal, Rowland Oliver, of whom more anon, offered more, but surprisingly, I got the nod. I was in the Cricket First XI for two years but was dropped before the end of the second season. I then starred when I was picked to tour with the First Eleven.

I aspired to play rugby in the 1stXV but got no higher than the 2nd team, and I'm not always in that- hardly a near miss! I was in the Hockey First XI but only intermittently, so it was a near miss. I was a good squash player and fancied my chances to win the School Squash Championship, but after a very close final, I was once again runner-up. I was selected for the School Drysdale Squash Cup team but lost my only game. I was a distant 3rd in the Annual School Cross Country Race. I auditioned for the lead role in the School's production of "Macbeth" but only got to play MacDuff, and in "Julius Caesar" the following year, I only managed to get to play the somewhat undistinguished part of 'Cinna the Poet.' A series of near misses.

One thing I absolutely and publicly detested at St Jude's was the application of discipline- the symbol of which was, as in the majority of Public Schools, the cane. In most schools, the cane was usually and frequently administered, often quite brutally, by masters. At St. Jude's, caning was, at least in part, literally in the hands of the Prefects via a process called the Prefects' Court, where offending boys were "tried" and' if found guilty, which they almost invariably were, then beaten by a Prefect. I could never forget the relish exhibited at the first caning I witnessed, which was also my last, administered by a thuggish Prefect- Bruce Carstairs, who clearly enjoyed himself thrashing a shrimp of a boy, apparently guilty of the heinous crime of running in the corridor, and who tried without success, to avoid crying or peeing.

The Prefects themselves, me amongst them, led school lives far from perfect- in the dead of the final night in the final week of our final term, led by one of our numbers, we took up every one of the 28 Masters' desks and swapped its site with another: 'a jolly prank' thought half the staff, 'We'll get the bastards and beat the living daylights out of them' thought the other half. "A very jolly prank," thought the Headmaster, when, to great applause, he smilingly reported on the event at our final assembly.

Chapter 2.

Being a Son

In this, we see JB fail to convince his family that he should head for University primarily in search of a Blue. But we do see him triumph in his burning desire to lose his virginity.

The evening after the Final Assembly was filled by a final Prefect's party with a few favoured guests- the Headmaster and his wife, a few other Masters, Ma Douglas, the much-loved School Cook, Charlie Staples, the Head Porter, and Andy Powell, the Head Groundsman – all united to say goodbye to a group of boys destined likely never to meet again, although fifty years on, this was to prove not to be the case.

Meanwhile, the Bright family had to give due thought and make up their united minds as to "What and where next for the youngest son/brother, Julian)" It was 1960, he was eighteen, about to leave school, a nearly successful schoolboy, clueless about the future, an innocent about to be abroad but without any actual 'foreign' experience, and a virgin (not a part of the family discussion). I was determined to address all these latter points: either my contemporaries were richer, luckier, better looking, or liars- they all seemed to have travelled, mostly to France, some to Spain, and two to the USA- I had never left these shores. They all claimed that they had slept with the girl or even girls of their choice. It was always "Terrific!" Mm! Perhaps.

In the holiday period immediately after I left school, I resolved to address these to me two big issues- travel and sex and to give them my full attention while my Mother and, to a lesser extent, my brothers also focused on the third: - University? If not to University, what instead and where? To which was added possible recruitment into the Armed Services or a normal sort of job?

I later confessed to having been thinking, "If university, which one, and what should I read? I was confident I should get into whichever university I chose - my A-Level results were good enough, and I had scored a few good points outside the classroom. I would probably get a grant from Croydon Council, which at that time would have been easy to obtain (it was, but as it turned out, it was never actually needed), and my still very much alive, bombed-out grandfather had promised his continued financial support. I had no interest in reading anything but English or History. But, to me, much more importantly, I had secretly been thinking seriously about the chances of getting a Blue: a Cricket Blue, or even two Blues, as I, not entirely just wishfully thinking, added Squash to my ambition. Each was possible, but both together were less likely. I thought I could, and probably should, get a cricket Blue. I was good enough generally, and right now, I was in very good form. I thought a squash Blue would be the icing on my personal cake, but once at University, there would be a lot of competition, so it was less likely more of a gamble. As to where I went, my personal choice would probably have been Wadham College, Oxford, where my father had gone, but I did not really get any say!

The School dealt with my first issue – travel. For the first time, it was decided that the Cricket First XI plus two or three reserves should go on an Overseas Tour. Holland was the chosen country. I had recently been dropped from the First team and, obviously, I was not held in much esteem by the Cricket Master, one Mr Pickles, so I was very far from sure that I would be picked but, in the end, I was selected and went, and, in fact, had a good tour, comfortably the most successful bowler and I, no mean batsman, hit a huge six on the Leiden ground, a bigger strike than anybody previously except for one Gary Sobers, a couple of seasons before.

I found I loved "abroad," especially Holland (and still do), and I rejoiced in the fact that I would never have to have any dealings with Pickles the Cricket Master once I had left school.

Now on to what to me was easily the most important matter: he felt he must address the sex issue, and this might be a real opportunity- "I am quite good-looking, I was quite self-confident, I had had lots of girlfriends. I did not have much money, but I could at least earn some of it by working for our local nursery gardener, a church friend of my Mother's.

All members of not only my immediate family but almost all my relatives on both sides of our extensive family and all age groups were active members of a church group called the Plymouth Brethren (of whom much more anon), which was something of a limiting hurdle in the girl area.

I had made several attempts to lose my virginity and was working assiduously to try and achieve this by having a series of girl-friends with whom I could, at the least, be proud to be seen out with, or, more ambitiously have a genuine chance to have sex with, ideally both. I had so far been consistently unsuccessful, but I was not about to give up.

And then…….my Mother had a very close unmarried friend called Linda Salter. Inappropriately, perhaps my Mother and Linda had met and became very good long-term friends initially through Brethren Meeting contacts, but my Mother, very supportive of all things Linda ever did, was quick to say how pretty Linda was and how sexy she was (My Mother was totally correct!). Another important but unusual factor was that Linda's parents were senior players in the Salvation Army.

Linda had, because of my Mother's friendship and influence, become involved, albeit gently, with the Plymouth Brethren and began attending their weekly Meetings. This was in 1953. Linda's parents were the only people we had ever known, let alone met, who actually owned a television set, flickering black and white, of course. It was at Linda's parents' house that my mother and I first watched television at all - it was on Saturday, 2nd June 1953, and it was very famous- the Coronation of Her Majesty Queen Elizabeth 11. For a colossal number of UK residents, this was the very first time they had watched television in their lives: my Mother and I were two of them.

Sometime after this, quite a long time actually, I realised I really rather fancied Linda but more like four years before I had a golden chance to do something about it, but fancy her I did- I was now seventeen! Linda had a good job, one which actually had a profound long-term commercial effect on me. She worked in advertising as the very influential PA to the Owner/Chief Executive of Paxton's, a medium-size, successful advertising agency based in Piccadilly. It is not particularly creative but reliable and relied upon, with a good client list and a good reputation. One of the Agency's more visible and talked-about Clients was 'Earl's Court' itself and all its shows and displays, including the very famous Royal Tournament.

Linda asked my Mother if she thought I would like to attend the Royal Tournament, where the Agency took a box every evening and provided drinks and canapes for a succession of the Agency's Clients and hangers-on like me. My mother thought that I would certainly be up for that, so a more formal invitation was issued. On the due date, I turned up at Linda's office a few yards from Piccadilly Circus on time and ready to go. Linda greeted me with a long face, an apology, and the need to postpone attending the Royal Tournament due to a mini-crisis with another Client. The Royal Tournament evening could be postponed and was. I think Linda might already have had a drink or two, and I was happy to agree to hang around while she finished dealing with the other Client crisis -then we could have a beer together.

A month or so later, while having another beer with the best of my friends, Roland Oliver, I told him how the evening had panned out. Julian said, "Absolutely impossible to remain untold." He then did the telling:

"She worked. I helped myself to a beer from her fridge and wandered round the rather dull offices. Linda's office was immediately outside her absent boss's predictably palatial office. While she worked hammering away at her type-writer, I wandered around the place, including having a nose around the boss's domain, where I got the shock of my life. In one corner of the grand office, there was a discreet, barely visible door, and I nosily but silently opened it. It was a small bedroom with an even smaller bathroom attached, but the really striking feature of the bedroom was that the walls were absolutely covered with hundreds of photos and pictures, every one of them very explicitly pornographic, the sort of stuff I had never seen before or been remotely aware of. By far, the most amazing thing was that a large number of the women's photos were of Linda either on her own, or very often with a man who I recognised as being her boss, or a few with another nude woman. They were absolutely sensational and very, very arousing. My reaction was immediate and predictable, and my next steps were instant. I took one of the sexiest photos of Linda on her own and went to her office. A startled look, a stifled scream, an unsuccessful attempt to seize the photo, and a demand to give her the photo at once and never to make any reference to it ever again either to her, certainly not to any member of our family, very especially, my Mother or any of the Paxton office colleagues. It was absolutely the biggest secret ever and was never to be told. I suggested a deal- I had never in my life seen a naked woman, but if she were to strip her clothes off, I would do the same to make it fair and, of course, not only give her the photo back but I would never mention anything about it, or the secret bedroom and certainly not the gallery of photos to anyone, very especially to my Mother. Her immediate reaction was unsurprisingly completely negative, and she made another futile attempt to seize the photo, but I was very much too quick for her, the more so as she had to circumnavigate her desk and, as I had thought, she had had a glass or two. I explained to her that if she did not cooperate, the first person I might share the photo with would be my Mother, her very best friend. I thought this was a timely moment to take all my clothes off, and the sight of a nude me seemed to stimulate Linda. Within seconds, there were two entirely nude people in the room, and within minutes, the same two were enjoying each other's very close proximity on the office sofa, and I was losing my virginity. I was eighteen, and Linda was thirty-six!

I must say this experience vastly exceeded my highest expectation, and so I made sure we continued this, which we duly did both in her office early in the evening when everyone had gone home and, quite frequently, in our house when my Mother and brothers were elsewhere. The affair stopped when Linda revealed that she was pregnant. She also revealed, but only, I think, to me, that the father could be either me, her boss, one other of the Agency Account Directors, or, very surprisingly, one of her parents' Salvation Army colleagues, and it was the latter lover who Linda married and with whom, in due time, raised a family while I had very happily resolved the now historical issue of my virginity. In fact, I thought I would like to see if I could find another Linda initially without giving up on the first one. This proved to be quite easy, the more so because it fitted Linda's plans, too. There was a family, Plymouth Brother friends of my mother's and Linda's, called Forester, with two daughters, Marie and Rose, who were both pretty and Marie rather the more curvaceous. Meeting her in a local wooded park, Lloyd's Park, I found she was interested in our getting to know each other a good deal more closely. So, we did. Often.

We both had dogs (the ostensible reason for trips to the Park), so we both had to deal with the problem of dog security. We found a discreet, overgrown clearing where we could be private and the two dogs could be tied up.

I thought that keeping my great, long-time friend, Rowland, up to speed on matters of the bed-room was a bounden duty. Rowland found it difficult to believe his friend's story, although, until the end, the bit about the dogs and their role in the Park, which in turn reminded him of one of the long-term truths in Bright family life- "One way in which their family life differed from most was the dominance of 'pets.' Led, as in most, all really, family matters by their Mother who had a pair of Cocker spaniels- Topsy and Turvy; Edmund Junior and Tim each had cats- Orlando and Peachy; Michael had, of all things, a caged parrot- John Silver; James had an aquarium, a large one, positively teeming with tropical fish, all unnamed. Julian had his beloved Red Setter- Handsome. "And now," Rowland told other friends, "Dogs are part of the Bright sex organisation team."

All the family, in a variety of ways, loved whatever was theirs and liked whatever was owned by the rest of the family, all the others. Organising their care and upkeep was a full-time business mostly carried out, of course, by my Mother, except for their Park duties and when we went to Cornwall each summer for the family holiday, which we did every year. Then Nanny Acock, Grandfather Olivier's housekeeper, would willingly and literally step in, and the dogs did not complain, and they were stood down from their Park roles.

Chapter 3.

Becoming a Man

The family conclave decided that it would not be University, it would not be the Army, Accountancy, or Media, but it would be Business.

My life and times with Linda and now others had, in my view, been huge steps forward in life, but they were just for me and not a part of my family's plan for my future. All the family felt they should concentrate on the important decision- making process of what I did next, which for them boiled down to going up to University or not, into Media or not, or the Armed forces or not, or, alternatively, settling down to 'Business,' Interestingly at this stage, no one, not even Michael, already an Accountant in the family practice, suggested Accountancy in Grandpa Bright's firm (to me, it would have been very much the worst option, but I expected some pressure from someone but got none. My family was all aware that any wish I had to go to University was not to study but to win one, possibly two 'Blues'- my long-term ambition. I hoped to introduce this as a good reason for my going to University, preferably but not necessarily Oxford, at the family meeting which my Mother had called for over lunch the next Sunday -Sunday Roast being sacrosanct family time- "to discuss Julian's future."

Our mother had not been up to university, and few ladies did so in the first half of the twentieth century. It was a pity; she was very bright and outstanding at almost all sports. Of my four brothers, two had been to University, and two had not. My Mother announced to the assembled company, which included my brothers' other halves that I had now been told that I would not be "going up" and that the search for gainful employment probably in the commercial world would start at the end of the Summer Term, three weeks away.

I think my Mother believed that at this family meeting, we should be able to unite in agreement as to what I was going to do or not to do and that one or other of my four brothers or, a good deal less likely, my departed father from his grave would extoll the virtues of whatever it was that he had taken up and I would follow these lines of thought with enthusiasm and commitment. I rather doubted whether anyone else in the room shared this optimism.

My brothers and I mostly got on really well together, apart from odd spats about left-over food, shortages of drink, or the famous family shrapnel row. We all tended to be supportive of each other, and we always supported our mother, whatever she did or said. Now that the subject of the day was me, I looked to them for help and guidance- "Yes, yes, but what should I actually do?" They took it in turns, the oldest first to advise

Edmund Junior is the oldest member of the family and is not a Uni man. Area Sales Manager with Olivier Timber (the family firm still run by my grandfather, Allen). Married to Margaret, father of two. Famed collector of not only shrapnel but rugby programmes. Kind, lazy, and unambitious, He thought I should either join the timber firm or possibly an Estate Agency.

Michael is also a non-Uni man but a qualified Accountant with Grandfather Bright's firm (my father's job, which he hated but which Mike liked). A career achiever. Engaged to Sue, another Accountant. Pleasant, unassuming couple. He, too, recommended what he was doing but thought I might prefer journalism. He also thought the Timber firm could be a possibility. –

James- Service Manager, VW Cars. Flashiest Bright. Car and girl are mad. Good cricketer. Loves eating out. Probably, my favourite brother- we liked much the same things. He supported the journalism idea but suggested approaching MCC or the FA for a sports-related job.

Tim, my youngest brother – a Modern Languages graduate, now a young Manager in the Unilever Graduate Scheme majoring in Marketing- by far the most academic and downright clever of my brothers, unashamedly ambitious, going out with gorgeous Daphne. Very funny.

I was glad for my brothers. I was glad they seemed happy and fulfilled in their jobs not one of which interested me at all.

My brightest brother, Tim, who, after sailing through Cambridge reading Modern Languages, perversely advised my Mother that University would be a waste of my time as I was most likely to enter the commercial world anyhow, which would not necessarily demand a degree but would look for evidence of a brain, an ambition to work hard and fast and some sort of personal review probably from school. She thought this made sense, and I found myself filling in forms created by The Public Schools Appointments Board and then queuing for a series of interviews with a wide variety of possible but not particularly attractive employers, who included Sainsbury's, Chubb, The Metal Box Company, the GPO, Beecham's, the BBC, Heinz and Mars- all of whom had Junior Management Training Schemes and all of whom had after an interview offered me a job except the only one that was of the slightest interest to me- the BBC, who courteously but firmly turned me down.

There were two other candidate employers- neither of which I had any interest in but had to tread around carefully. My deceased father had reluctantly qualified to take and pass the necessary exams to join and work for his father's Chartered Accountancy firm, and I had to watch my step as this grandfather, Alfred Bright, exerted a lot of pressure on both my Mother and me to follow my father and my brother into the family practice. Michael, in fact, had done this much to their mutual satisfaction. My Mother's father, Allen Olivier, the generous grandparent who ran Oliviers, the family timber firm, supported me in the battle to avoid Accountancy, the very thought of which makes me retch to this day, a battle which we won, but he also had another motive and was inclined to press-gang me into Olivier Timber alongside Edmund Junior. Steps to be watched here, too, but I was able to avoid both, thanks to some wise words from my brother, Tim.

A second option for me was a more attractive possibility- the Army. Compulsory National Service had only just come to an end, but all three Services were still actively recruiting. I was interested- the pay was quite good, there was the opportunity for considerable travel (I still had only been on one trip, the Dutch cricket tour), and first-class sports facilities were available. I had what I thought was a promising interview at Aldershot, but sadly, it came to nothing because, rather embarrassingly, I failed the medical test, which was a compulsory part of the entrance process.

We reached the end of the family lunch, and all the various players had their say. This was where I realised that although every member of the family knew how keen I was to attend University with the sole ambition of getting a Blue, this topic had not had any sort of an airing at the family meeting. Even when I floated the thought towards the end of our chat, it was as though I had not spoken and we should "keep the meeting going as we are nearly done." Another half-hour and we were done- bang had gone University, and bang had gone the Blues.

Chapter 4.

Being a Brother

At the same sort of time as the Bright family was deciding on my future and that this would not include University, another round of decision-making was being forced on the whole family with huge consequences for all of them.

I already had not just four physical brothers, but the first twenty or so years of his life were dominated by his family's swamping involvement with religion, not just loads of immediate blood relatives but literally thousands of other Brothers and Sisters worldwide, a very strict Protestant sect called the Plymouth Brethren. But, as we shall see, tables were turned- the Plymouth Brethren disintegrated as a reputable Christian Sect, and its beliefs stood on their holy heads and life for the Bright family, for most of their extended family, and for many of their friends in the UK and around the world life was completely and utterly changed.

Both sides of my family- the Brights, led by my accountant grandfather, Alfred, and the Oliviers, led by my very generous and supportive grandfather, Allen, the timberman, and my Mother's father - were committed, active Protestant Christians, members of this sect variously known as the

Plymouth or the Exclusive Brethren. This was founded by a Church of England curate named John Nelson Darby in 1848 as a very strict, bible-based fellowship starting unsurprisingly in Plymouth. Now, just over one hundred years on, the Brethren have grown considerably with about 35,000 brothers and sisters with 'Meetings' as their Churches were called, spread internationally and particularly strong in the USA, Australia, and the UK. The Meetings were usually held in halls often rented from local churches: the members themselves, abstemious and abstaining, bible-led supported by sung but unaccompanied hymns, the services themselves, an hour or two long, and with an intense focus on Sunday Holy Communions with mid-week meetings for Prayer and, separately, for Bible Readings.

The Brethren were a dour, rather humourless sect. The men - the Brothers – tended mostly to wear blue suits and did so unfailingly on Sundays, almost always with trilby hats. The women, 'Sisters,' whether or not they actually were or were not blood relations, were encouraged (told) to grow their hair long and to wear it in 'buns' and then, rather pointlessly, expected always to wear hats. The Sisters were not allowed to participate in any of the Services, of which there were normally five every week- three on Sunday, one each on Monday and Thursday evenings. Brethren were not permitted to own televisions or radios. They were forbidden to go to the cinema, to the theatre, or a concert. They were discouraged from going to pubs. They were only to marry other Brethren. There were breaks in the boredom – I discovered a pair of Sisters (in real life and in their PB Church), Marie and Jill Forbes, whose house backed on to our local recreation ground, the familiar Lloyd's Park, and whose idea of recreation, I discovered, matched mine. We met quite frequently, and I was introduced to troilism.

Within the Brethren, especially the Exclusive Brethren, the sub-sect with which our family was entwined, leadership was regarded as key, and to a degree, nepotism was not just acceptable but encouraged. In the USA, the Taylor family, father then son, 'ruled' from 1959 to 1970. In Australia, the Hales ruled supremely, and still do - Bruce Hales, supported by his brothers and his belligerent sons, has stood as International Leader and "Elect Vessel" since 2002. In the UK, certainly in the South, my grandfather Allen Olivier was a sort of benign dictator.

The latter years of the Taylors were coloured by rather exciting rumours of alcoholism and sexual misbehaviour accompanied by stories of curious practices and questionable behaviour even while preaching. More significantly, James Taylor Junior, during the latter years of his leadership, introduced the practice of 'Separatism from the world.' This included the banning of eating with non-Brethren; not belonging to non-Brethren organisations; no membership of professional bodies; the forbidding of marriage to non-Brethren partners, and refusal to allow younger Brethren access to Universities. He also confusingly preached a relaxed view of drinking alcohol, especially Scotch, and his acceptance of more easy-going attitudes extended to his feeling free to sleep with 'a member of his flock' and to doing so very openly. He was very firm in enforcing "Taylorite" teaching on an international basis. It has to be said that some of us younger brothers found JT's views on sex and Scotch quite attractive but not seriously enough to follow suite.

In 1960, as a result of Separatism, the 'Church' of the Plymouth Brethren imploded. Chaos ensued as a mighty schism shook the Brethren world. "Meetings" closed down all over the world. Families broke up. Marriages failed, and friendships fell apart.

The majority of members of Plymouth Brethren 'Meetings' were truly horrified. Most simply could not live or certainly not worship within this new teaching from this unacceptable leadership, which they called "Taylorite." Thousands of the members worldwide resigned, and almost all moved churches, the majority to mainstream established gatherings. There were incidents of suicide, of murder, and a great deal of total religious back-sliding, and of giving up any form of 'Church' altogether.

As previously mentioned, the Olivier family, led by my grandfather, Allen, dominated London and the South, and such dominance was totally accepted by his 'flock.' But this mighty upheaval caused my grandfather to step down quietly and hand the local leadership over to an impressively ordinary Taylorite successor.

With the exception of a few unthinking cousins, our own extended family, led by both grandfathers, resigned from the Brotherhood. Not with a bang nor with a whimper, we all simply left. We ceased any form of attendance at the "Taylorite" meetings and, in most cases, looked for and found acceptable alternatives fairly quickly. Grandpa Olivier was in a strong position which he took considerable pleasure in exploiting. When he was informed by the Taylorites in his Croydon Meeting that he had been the equivalent of excommunicated, he rose to his feet. My grandfather was a big man in every way- he stood 6' 5". He was a broad man without an ounce of surplus fat on him. He invariably physically dominated any room, hall, or church. This was such an occasion.

He pointed out – he had a very strong, resonant voice, very good for effective 'pointing-out- and reminded the company, about 200 strong- that he personally owned the Coombe Street Hall where they were assembled; it was entirely his, and when he came to die, his two sons and their four sisters would inherit it under the terms of his will. His lawyer had accompanied him this evening and would be ready to vouchsafe all the legal points covering what needed to be known, but what could be said then, and there is that all those who did not wish to remain in fellowship with him, his family and his friends but wished to support James Taylor Junior should pack up their personal belongings and leave the building within thirty minutes. He also gently reminded the congregation that there were seven Brethren meeting-rooms in Croydon, and he owned them all. He would, he said, be grateful if someone from amongst the Taylorite group could take on the responsibility of advising the elders at all the meeting-rooms to vacate them by 1st February for certain and to pay all rent arrears by the same date.

So they, the Taylorites, left, mostly never to be seen or contacted again by their erstwhile brothers and sisters, and Allen Olivier and his family provided an immediate sumptuous tea for all who chose to remain. He then spoke for about fifteen minutes about how the reborn meeting would run. This started and finished with a short but somewhat emotional prayer meeting. That was it as far as 'The Peebs' and I were concerned, but the Taylorites felt my "devil-led" departure must not be allowed to go unpunished - alongside my grandfather's farewell speech. Both were to be publicly condemned. I was, therefore, subjected to a Brotherly visit to expel me formally and unforgivingly. A group of five brothers were given this fatuous task. The visit perhaps did not have the impact it might have done because I was due at a party, and my mates cruised up and down outside in their car, hooting the night away, waiting to take me away. I made the party, but it was a miss for the doleful Taylorites. My grandfather was also visited and given a totally meaningless 'sentence,' which made the big man laugh before showing his visitors the door.

As Grandfather Olivier could do no wrong in family eyes, there was little likelihood of any of us siding with the Taylorites, but we found ourselves somewhat forced to take sides, as in Croydon, where we lived, a considerable number of people who we had known all our lives, had decided to follow James Taylor and consequently would have nothing further whatsoever to do with us. Another group stayed friendly with us but opted to join Churches much more orthodox than any form of Brethrenism. Many immediately joined the Anglican Church, others became Baptists, and a large number dropped out of church altogether. Mostly, these moves created little social upheaval, and old friends remained friends. But the Taylorites behaved aggressively and would have little or nothing to do with their erstwhile fellow-Brethren, and a good number of families were split up and permanently so for so-called Christian reasons. The schism of the early 1960s remains a schism sixty years later. Families found themselves sundered, and very long-standing friendships and relationships fell apart. This was not a bloody war of destruction or land-grab, but it was a war of attitude and beliefs, and there were significant losses in terms of people and their relationships with each other, all in the name of Christianity. We lost one young friend separated from his parents, who took his own life in his own oven. Another whole family was shot by a demented father. Our family hung together well, but many close friends and some distant cousins suffered the misfortunes of this Holy War. Surprisingly, the original blameworthy leaders, Taylor and Hales, survived and re-emerged as the two world leaders.

Life in the Brethren had its amusing moments.

In the following days, there was some news totally unrelated to the Taylorite affair, but it was a true tale of one of the things that happened next in the fractured mess of PBism. It also made us laugh. My grandfather, a sort of local squire, during the latter stages of his life, had two families, the Bunkers and the Acock sisters, who tended the Olivier needs for most things in and around the house and garden, particularly the garden: the Acocks worked entirely in the house cooking and cleaning. The three strong Bunker family were Alfred, the gardener, Maud, and Martha were, the house-maids - they had been employed by the Oliviers for many years, and they were committed Plymouth Brethren, but they were all very old and were almost certainly unaware of what was currently going on. Very suddenly, Martha died, and Allen Olivier took on the responsibility of caring for her funeral. He recruited a Brethren (non-Taylorite) team to conduct the burial service. The team included four ex-Brethren pall-bearers - a local doctor, a local Nursery Gardner, a Bunker nephew, and me. Two of the bearers were vertically challenged, really very small men. The nephew and I were both about 6'- the unevenness of the carrying party was very noticeable and very comical, but no one seemed to mind. In fact, they laughed. The following week, at another Brethren funeral, two of the pallbearers were identical twin brothers burying their uncle, a very well-known shoe shoe-designer/maker. At the given word, the pallbearers set off towards the grave. It was unfortunate that two of the four set off south and two set off north. The coffin fell noisily but appropriately to earth; the coffin lid fell off, and the corpse sprang into a sitting position. Once more, mirth was induced. At this particular funeral, further laughter was generated when one worthy, surprisingly a Taylorite, Fulcher by name, got stuck in the lavatory, and by the deliberately extended time it took to release him, all the 'wake' food had been eaten, and the drink drunk (no alcohol) and all the funeral guests had mourned, had departed and had gone.

The Brethren were, and I think still are, individually quite wealthy, and this could be seen in the area of staff: lots of Brethren households seem to be able to afford considerable support- housekeepers, maids, au pairs, gardeners, and cleaners. Although we, as a family, had no money, my Mother had a cleaner- Ethel Watkins, an au pair- Trudi from Switzerland, a gardener – Chris Vickers, then Cyril Lancaster, and a weekly sewer/mender, Maud (actually Maud Emily

Martha) Pease. Not surprisingly, this left her with even less money.

I love anything that makes me laugh, especially when I am in the wrong place or, at the wrong time, or both. Laughter in Church has double potency because it is both rare and often frowned upon as inappropriate. Hence the glee at the two funerals, and I further remember one particular instance where a large percentage of the congregation was rendered helpless with laughter when the rather stout and elderly sidesman took up the collection one Sunday morning, with a full congregation and a very full collection basket, tripped over an errant hassock, fell and on the way down upturned the very full basket crowning a nearby, seated parishioner with its entire contents to the entire joy of everyone in the Church including the Vicar.

I further remember one specific and triumphant incident, a sort of set piece carefully planned and carefully executed in the latter days of the Plymouth Brethren as I knew them. The local Brethren, mostly from South London and the Home Counties, had a massive 'meeting' at what is now the Fairfield Halls, Croydon. The main hall was absolutely packed, and silence was total as we all waited for the arrival of the great man himself- James Taylor, called by his flocks worldwide with the utmost respect, JT Junior. He was due to arrive any minute in a chauffeur-driven limousine to address the assembled throng. He did indeed arrive to a tumultuous welcome, cheering and clapping, as he headed for the podium from which he would speak. As he walked down the aisle, he was flanked by two local worthies, obviously his 'minders' and, wait a minute, he was also accompanied by a uniformed police officer, a suited man looking like a Council official (which is exactly what he was and probably is), and two dungareed men clearly carrying bags of tools (actually me and my very best friend, Alastair Rowling). The four reached the podium, and the Council Official (also a departing PB) called for silence. The seated crowd of several hundred was inclined to ignore him until the Policeman stepped forward and raised a hand and, with a stentorian voice, demanded silence. JT Junior joined him in successfully hushing the crowd.

The Council Man, one Richard Beecham, advised that the "meeting could not take place." He was sorry, but "The Hall must be evacuated immediately" as it was "too dangerous to go ahead because a gas leak has been identified" and, pointing to the dungareed pair, "These gentlemen are here to try to fix the problem as quickly as possible but insist on the Hall being cleared into the Car Park at once. It is likely to take some hours to find and solve the problem and to make the Hall safe again."

Senior Brethren, perhaps for the first time experiencing a dose of nearlyism for their major Meeting, rapidly ushered JT Junior out and bundled him into his car, which his chauffeur (my brother Tim) drove to his hotel. Our friend, Chris Farnes, meanwhile slipped out of his hired police uniform and joined the Council Official and us, the two dungareed men, in the pub, knowing there was not a leak, nor had there ever been, and there was now no meeting either. This small team of fakes adjourned to "The Swan and Sugar Loaf," a local Croydon pub, rather hoping that JT Junior might join them as not only was the range of Scotches impressive, but they were joined by Jenny Carr, whose main claim to sisterly fame was that she had been caught in bed with JT Junior, a much publicised and recent event, and it seemed she was scheduled to have a post- meeting date with the great man.

He failed to show.

Chapter 5.

Being in "fresh woods and pastures new"

The turmoil of the schism destroying the Plymouth Brethren, followed by the two funerals, at which the attendance of all my family was mandatory, left me with something of a problem- I had no church, and I wanted a replacement social life. A helpful uncle steered me in a promising direction – "Try St. Barnabas, an active, lively Church with a strong young people's section. You'll love it"." He had, it transpired made a good suggestion, and I made a good decision when I joined it.

It was basically a local Anglican Church that focused mainly on younger people mostly in their early twenties, with a fresh and, to an ex-Plymouth Brother like me, compelling program, a mixture of Church Services and social events of which there was a very active program including something that sounded interesting called "The Twenty-Forty Club," which, in turn, was a mixture of Christian activity and a busy social and sporting program. I joined this and became an active member, attending most of the religious gatherings, albeit not particularly enthusiastically, and many of the social activities. There were evening cricket matches, tennis and squash tournaments, barbecues, dancing, and simple parties, a lot of it right up my street

It so happened that when I joined "The Twenty-Forty Club," they were about to hold their annual birthday party, their fifth but, obviously, my first. We all paid our own way, not cheap at £50 a head, but all the drink was donated by a family called Mainwaring, very obviously influential and generous members. He, it turned out, was a very successful Lloyd's broker, and she owned and ran a high-end dress shop. We milled around being very well fed from a flotilla of trays borne by a bevy of professional waiters carrying loads of upmarket and very imaginative snacks, vineyards of endless wine, and with everyone, including me, very coolly dressed. I was unashamedly on the hunt, and there seemed to be a lot of talent around and available, but I did not know a soul.

Then there they were! Two of the prettiest girls certainly in this room, possibly in the world - one was brunette, slim and pretty, while the other was raven-haired and with an eye-catching figure of the sort called 'fuller.' It looked like they might be sisters (they were); it looked as if they were unaccompanied (but then so was I). Who might introduce me? God stepped in.

I cannot really dance, but I can pretend with the best of them. I can sort of jive, and I am not shy. The two girls looked unaccompanied, and I approached confidently and suggested we create a threesome and went for it. I told them, "I am Julian Bright. I am new here, and I regret to say that dancing is not one of my strengths". Brunette/slim was up for it, but seemed likely to be too good a dancer. She told me her name was Fiona MacIntyre, and her sister was Roanna. If it had been a free choice, I would have set my sights and a lot more of me on Roanna, but I felt instinctively that I had so far failed to bowl her over. In contrast, Fiona had edged physically nearer to me - in fact, she was holding my left arm quite tightly while Roanna hovered alongside, not touching me at all.

So, I found myself in, I thought, a thoroughly enviable situation. I spent the whole party chatting up the MacIntyre girls, comfortably the two best-looking girls at the party and seemingly content with my company not, it turned out, just that evening but fairly frequently with one or both of them at either church functions (rarely and not particularly enthusiastically attended), or parties like the Twenty-Forty one, (always pretty good but always the same people each time), but also quite a lot of movies and concerts given by the hot bands of the time- 'The Searchers,' 'Sonny and Cher,' and, best of all, 'The Stones' at Earls Court. Everything so so different from the sort of entertainment the 'Peebs' permitted.

The MacIntyres lived in some style on their own; both parents had died the year before, and they enjoyed entertaining. Both were goodish cooks, and they gave parties and dinner parties quite regularly. I was almost always on the guest list and looked after the drinks. If I had to decide between the two of them, I would have selected Roanna – they were both very good-looking, but Roanna was sexier. But I didn't have to make a decision; I just had to steer a careful, inoffensive path between them. This was not too difficult as they worked in different places and did different things. Fiona worked for the very cool Lynch Shoe company in Oxford, and Roanna worked for Vogue in London - And they had quite different interests – Fiona was a keen, competent sportswoman and, not surprisingly, Roanna was deeply into fashion, obsessively so in fact.

I was very keen to have sex with either or, better, both of them, but it was not to be. One evening, I thought I was about to succeed - Fiona and I were alone, and Roanna was out on a date. I had managed to remove all Fiona's upper clothing and was positioning myself for further disrobing when Roanna's unexpectedly early return destroyed my plans. My reaction, perhaps an unwise one, was to laugh, Roanna's was to rage, and Fiona's to blush rather than cry. If ever there was an example of "a nearly man" this sadly was it. I never saw either of them again and felt it made sense for me to move on from the Twenty-Forty Club to look elsewhere for a girlfriend and yet another social life. A funny period in my life, one of the 'nearliest' experiences of my life, but rather a sad one, really.

I, therefore, needed to spend a while looking for another new Church, most likely Anglican. Still, there was always the possibility of sticking loyally to the Alan Olivier Church, which I thought, quite rightly as it turned out, would be very much like the pre-Taylorite Exclusive Church (but freer). I tried the Baptists; I tried the cool HTB Church in Brompton, and even went to one Pentecostal Service in Shepherd's Bush, rather good, actually, and literally upbeat.

In the meantime, my life and career were progressing satisfactorily, the more so once I had left the Plymouth Brethren. Much was new in these early stages of my adulthood: a new job doing precisely what I had always wanted to do and making me pretty well-off, newly freed up from a Church point of view but now with a new social life to be created.

Chapter 6.

Becoming a worker

After school, work. Six years in my first with a fine company and, it seemed to me, a very good start to what I hoped would become a decent career. I was right. My second job was as much a change of discipline as a company- Manufacturing to Marketing - Metal Box to Cheseborough-Ponds. Ponds to Grey-Advertising, again a deliberate discipline move. On to Bright & Partners and finally, just me, in the somewhat misleading The Bright Partnership.

The first of the companies that had offered me a job was Metal Box of whom, until I was invited to attend one of their offices in Southwark for an initial interview, I must confess I had never heard. I was invited to come back for a second interview. I met and was interviewed by Jim Waterman, Head of Personnel- a charming man and, as I discovered very quickly, outstandingly good at his job. We talked through the details of the Junior Management Training Program, what my first job would be, what I would be paid- (£450 a year!), where I would work (Acton), and how I could expect my career with Metal Box to pan out. He really got through to me, we got on famously, and then, and there, I accepted the job offer. We became and remained the firmest of friends for some twenty years, by which time he had retired, and I was a high-flying adman.

This, my first job, started at the end of August 1960. It was an awful ninety-minute daily commute from South Croydon to West Acton. I very much enjoyed the six years I worked for Metal Box; in fact, they were important years much my growing up years. In all honesty, I probably would have preferred to have joined either the BBC or the Army, but that was not to be. I found a job which I liked, with people I liked even more. Without exception, I found the people I worked with and for tremendous-great fun and highly professional. I did well, and my money increased. Jim Waterman kept an eye on me, and I was moved around the country and up the ladder quite quickly in a way that very much suited a young bachelor both professionally and socially.

Metal Box was a paternalistic organization with factories and offices all around the country and in many places overseas. Every unit was exceptionally well equipped – with well-furnished, comfortable offices. They all had good sports facilities, usually cricket- and football pitches, and included indoor activities like billiard tables, table tennis, and bowling-alleys. Almost all of them had bars and good dining facilities serving somewhat less good food.

A very memorable first day- I was shown to my desk by my new boss. The desk was big, shared by two of us. My first working partner was black, a Nigerian. I had never in my life so far met or spoken to a black person, not at school, not in our Church, nor in any sport I had played. Bibi, the Nigerian, was a terrific bloke, and we became real mates and kept in touch for years. The younger men in the office always played football during the lunch break; Bibi was a star, much better than me. For me, this remained a hugely important experience, a totally positive one, and it proved to be a great start and important over time.

Two years on. My first move came quickly and completely out of the blue and turned out to be very well worthwhile. Bibi had gone home to MB Nigeria, and I had moved away from the double desk to a glass-walled office where three of us had desks and from whence we could see out over the other twenty or so desks, and they could look in to see what we might or might not be at. We were over-staffed. We did not have very much to do and so did not do it. It was a Friday, usually the quietest day of the working week, and we were expecting to break for lunchtime football as usual in about thirty minutes. I was preparing for this by reading whatever my current book was; I can actually remember it - "And Berry Came Too" by Dornford Yates (that's what my memory used to be able to do!). A tap on the glass. The very top man, the General Manager, one Mr. Jeff Wighall, came in and, spoke to me for the first time, possibly also the last time.

"You haven't got time to be reading a book."

Cheekily and dangerously, I replied that I rather thought I had got the time. I advised Mr. Wighall with total accuracy that I had always finished my weekly work by Thursday morning. I said that Thursday afternoons were always spent organizing whatever the needs were of The Metal Box Acton Skittles League– a weekly task thrust upon me by a majority of my office colleagues because of my obvious spare time, contributing to other inter-factory activities and Friday afternoons would finish the week with my running a Two- Hour Staff Fitness Training Program for any of the office staff or factory-workers, who liked to attend. This always finished in the Acton site bar for a pint or two and sometimes a getting-to-know-you session with one of the friendly secretaries in an empty office.

Arthur Knowles, one of the more senior Managers and a seriously good footballer, a Blue in fact, who shared the glass-house with me and one other, James Glass, spoke up to confirm that all three of us invariably finished our week by Thursday evening and very rarely had any work to do on a

Friday. "Not even Skittles?" said Jeff Wighall, who, it must be said, was very friendly and chatty, clearly very interested in what we had to say. He then talked a bit about a job, a good job as Production Controller of a newly opened factory in Arbroath, Scotland. We knew a number of experienced, therefore older, Acton colleagues had applied eagerly for this post, but, so far, none of them had been offered the job. Jeff Wighall suggested we had a beer together at the end of the day, which we duly and enjoyably did, although I thought at the time that there was an element of the interview in our conversation.

On the following Monday morning, I was called by Jeff. Wighall's office, I assumed that this would be the time when I might get something of a lambasting following the reality and informality of the previous idle Friday's natter. Nothing could be further from the truth; he invited me to apply for the Arbroath job. I was 20! I was given a return train ticket for the next day and a note from Gerry Thwaites, Manager of the Arbroath factory, saying he would like to see me on the morrow, Tuesday, in Scotland to be interviewed for the Production Controller's job. I was offered the job on Wednesday and approved on Thursday – "one of your working days, Julian?" – by the man I now called Jeff. I started there on Monday, ten days later, to my considerable pleasure and somewhat to the chagrin of many of my much more experienced Acton colleagues, who had applied for but not gotten the job and who found it difficult to accept that I had just twenty, with very little experience in the Company, had got what was a plum job, (probably because I had then had and have to this day, still got the gift of the gab). Meanwhile, at home, my mother was experiencing mixed emotions – pride at my early promotion and sorrow at my relocation.

I worked in Scotland for two great years, and I did pretty well.

-the factory ran efficiently and productively, I was a 'boss' for the first time at only twenty and I had developed a couple of good relationships with Scottish girls. One was Leila, a nurse at Arbroath's hospital, who conveniently had a small flat, and the other was Sheena, who worked in my factory but rather oddly liked, when out on a date, to wear curlers in her hair.

Home matches with Sheena took place in her mother's house. In the evening, when the mother was a barmaid in the local pub. I also nearly had an affair, real but rather brief, with a married MB manager, who I thought was to be the love of my life. I was wrong by quite a distance, but it was fun, as near misses often are.

My final two years with Metal Box were spent in Worcester- a very good job managing a department and earning significantly more money in a lovely city. A major bonus linked to the job was my being asked to run the Metal Box Worcester Girl's Netball team, a promotion from the Acton Skittles League- they were very good at netball. They won every competition they entered, but certainly not because of my contribution as Manager. Another personal bonus was that they were also, in the main, very good-looking, and it seemed one of my duties was to look after them closely. One disappointment was that I thought that, once again, I was going to marry one of them, and I nearly did, but this was again not to be. I think she was the Goal Shooter. She also met someone else. I went to her wedding and finished up late on with her very attractive mother under the table, which bore the carcass of the cake. A few weeks later, Metal Box returned me to London, to a new job, a new home and sadly single. I thought I was about to be appointed Manager of one of Metal Box's smaller units in Speke. I nearly got it, but at the last minute, the plug was pulled on the appointment, and an older and senior member already on the local staff was promoted, probably fairly but disappointing.

When I remember the time I spent in Worcester, I do so with great affection., I had a great time at work- a very good new job which I had first to create and then manage, my own Department with good, young people, clear objectives, a mixture of hard work and fun, and a great time socially. Metal Box Worcester was closely involved with Worcester Cricket Club, County Champions, for the two years I was living there. It was also the city in which I met my wife.

I rented the wing of a biggish manor house in Kempsey, a village just outside the city. The house was perfect for parties, especially when the County Cricket team was playing at home and looking for post-cricket action. Our more regular guests included Dick Richardson (a top batter/fielder), Tom Graveney (a world-class batsman), Jim Standen (a great fielder and a greater goal-keeper at West Ham and great fun), and Basil D'Oliveira (another world-class Test Player).

My time with Metal Box was coming to an end for a number of positive reasons, but mostly because I felt I needed to think about broadening my career. I had started my working life in Manufacturing, and I felt I needed to extend my experience. Although I knew nothing about it, the cool area seemed to be Marketing, so I set my sights on this discipline but to do so, I needed to get back to London.

I had rather lost touch with both Jim Waterman, who retired early and now lives in Greece near where the Leigh Fermors famously lived, and Jeff Wighall, whose first wife divorced, then remarried a very pretty Metal Box girl and got a very big job somewhere in the rag trade, but he did not invite me to his wedding perhaps because he knew that I had been very close to his new wife at an earlier time. Both men were really very important to launching and then furthering my career, and I still hold both in great respect and gratitude. I would be very happy to buy them a classy drink or even two.

The new job was a deliberate, planned transfer from working in Manufacturing in the three different MB factories I had worked in, mostly making rather dull cans, to what seemed a much cooler sector- Marketing- and to do this with a well-known American toiletry and cosmetic company- Cheseborough-Pond's, a good deal sexier and more talked about than the world of tin cans.

I started life with Pond's, still in a Manufacturing role but acting as a sort of bridge between making and marketing, with my eyes set on becoming a full-time member of the Marketing Team.

I was able to slip into the Marketing function firstly in London, then in Dublin back to London again, a time I thoroughly enjoyed apart from two 'nearly' events.

Then Pond's gave me my great, life-changing chance. A vacancy occurred in their Irish Marketing Department based in Dublin, and they offered me a Brand Manager's job. I accepted it with alacrity. I had become a Marketer.

Chapter 7.

Being in Ireland But Not Irish

Everything changes for the better. The new work discipline proves to be a very good move. Socially, Dublin is a winner, and our man plays a lot of good cricket.

I loved Ireland, I loved Dublin, I loved the Irish people, especially the high cheek-boned Irish girls I worked and played with, and I loved my new job and perhaps above all, I loved my new boss- Dan Wenham – he became a great friend and proved to be an outstanding teacher.

I started life in Ireland with a few weeks in the Montrose Hotel. I started my charm offensive among Irish girls with the beautiful Christina and Bridget, the hotel's Receptionists.

I found an excellent flat on the seafront at Dun Laoghaire, which was a twenty-minute drive from my office. The office, in turn, was under ten minutes from Rathmines, Leinster's cricket ground. I joined this club and had a couple of very productive seasons, in the first of which we won the main Club trophy partly because I got a lot of wickets. Still, we won mostly because of the presence of Ireland's best bowler, Gerry Duffy, a star spinner and a great man.

I went to Dublin not knowing a soul and rather worried about how this might affect my chance with Irish girls about whom I had heard nothing but good things up to, not necessarily including sex. I need not have worried. I fell in love with a local pub – the Queen's Head in Dalkey – and I went there a lot. It was there I discovered a strange but helpful Irish male habit: Irish men take their girls to the pub, provide them with the drinks of their choice, then sit them all down in a semi-circle about fifteen feet from the bar while the men themselves remain at the bar to natter with their mates. It was very easy for a cool, lone wolf such as I was to cruise around the girls in their half-circle chatting up, then stealing, the most obviously available with some ease. I met in; I think, the correct order- Christina, Ita McGillyreddy (prize for the best name),

Sandy Anson, the Hallworthy sisters, Lara and Beatrice, and many others, all stars. I failed to meet any of their chaps but I personally had a marvellous time.

I needed to make a fast, visibly active start to performing in my new job and to impress my new work-mates firstly by taking steps to find out just what 'Marketing' actually meant and what I was expected to do and then doing it well. This I did with reasonable swiftness with some telephonic help from my brother, Tim, some excellent tuition and guidance from my boss, Dan, a superstar in his own right, and, let it be said, my new, thoroughly supportive workmates. My very good memory proved to be an excellent thing to have.

I vividly remember my first Ad Agency meeting in Arks, regarded rightly to be one of Ireland's top Agencies. A guy called Roger had just made an involving presentation about Arks and the work the Agency had done or was doing for Ponds. We were breaking for a tea break when the door opened, and in flew a ragged elderly crone; she eyed the big, shiny board-room table around which we were all sitting and on which there was a handsome box full to the brim with cigarettes, Carroll's, who I later learned was another Agency client.

Without a nanosecond's hesitation, the crone dived full length and rather elegantly onto the shiny, slippery table and skidded its length 15 feet or so, scooping up all the cigarettes on her way through, flew off the table at its far end and out of the door that ends, on to Harcourt Street, an important Dublin thoroughfare. In no time at all, she was gone. It took several minutes for our meeting to recover and then regain some momentum. The more senior Agency staff were visibly embarrassed, and everyone else was crying with laughter.

My flat looked onto Dun Laoghaire Harbor, in fact, to the Yacht Club, and I often crewed on our Sales Company's racing yacht. I particularly recall one regatta day. I was on board with a further four yachty people but it was completely windless. Progress was not slow; it was non-existent. We had two or three cases of canned beer, on which we actually concentrated our attention for most of the afternoon. We sailed or, actually, did not sail an inch except as the tide took us but we did drink the beer. When the Committee boat came out to tow all the 'racing' boats back to very close to my front door, we counted all the empty cans that we could see, most of which we had thoughtlessly tossed into the sea around us. We hoicked them back on board; they totalled seventy-two!

My time in Dublin came to an end when Dan, General Manager and my truly excellent friend and boss, was promoted to what was seen as one of the top jobs in the Company - Sales and Marketing Director of the UK company- and he took me with him.

All the time I had spent in Ireland I had never come across one iota of anti-Englishness. The reverse – I was made nothing but very welcome, very included, and had a great deal of pleasure and fun. It was not until my last night in Dublin that suddenly everything changed in a sour fashion.

I threw a farewell party in the cricket Pavilion at Rathmines.

There was a second party going on in the Upper Room of the same Pavilion. Someone's birthday, nothing to do with cricket. But when The Upper Room discovered that I was English, which displeased them greatly, they tried to manhandle me out of my own party and promised to keep man-handling me onto a plane or a boat the following morning. I was not planning to leave for a week or so, but I kept this quiet. My friends and supporters leaped to the rescue with immediate success, possibly because we significantly outnumbered the battling birthday celebrants, and it seemed that we were a lot fitter.

Gerry Duffy, very well known by everybody and very much liked and admired by all in both rooms, called for silence and handshakes, and he got them almost instantly. The birthday guy and I had a drink together, and that was that. An unpleasant incident that happily ended harmoniously.

A pity that it did end like that, though, a jarring note. But I go back to Ireland as often as I can, and I count one Irish family, as it happens to be a past client, as one of my dearest friendships anywhere, not just in Ireland. I thought my career would develop in Dublin. Still, I was pipped at the proverbial post by an Irish colleague of distinctly lower calibre and I had had another nearly experience. He was moved on as a failure after six months, but by then, I too had moved back to London, where I had another rebuff when the Marketing Director's job there became vacant, but the Sales Director was given both jobs- another nearly one.

However, 1969 became an important year for very different reasons- I was Best Man at a good friend's wedding in Worcester Cathedral, at which I met and subsequently married my wife, Emma. We chose to marry on 4th July 1970, curious perhaps, it being Independence Day- a very significant life change. A new job, a new home, a new wife, then new children- then, rather later, grandchildren of our own, all in reasonable harmony with ups and downs but mostly ups.

Chapter 8.

Being in London, capital of the Ad world

The changes experienced going to and living in Dublin had been immense. Going back to London was even more different. New job discipline, marriage, and our first house.

I was back home, but, more importantly, I was lining myself up for my last big career move. I was going to fulfil my greatest ambition. I was absolutely determined to become an Ad Man and to do so as soon as I could. It took a while but in due course, I did.

I loved my time in Marketing. It was an excellent opportunity to combine diagnostic thinking with creative execution (pompous fool!). For me, the job was my first real experience within the creative world, where, in effect, I stayed for the next fifty years. There was another more practical plus point when I moved back to the Pond's London Marketing Department - I became entitled to a company car. But a bigger reason for entering and staying in Marketing revealed itself once I had got my feet under the desk or on the car pedals, which was that you were in frequent contact, certainly most Fridays after work or, possibly, after lunch, with a familiar breed of person, who was "The Agency," I had, of course, had considerable contact with such folk at Arks in Dublin, and with the Paxton Agency where Linda had worked and played but this was the real thing with London agencies.

Marketing, London was a very different kettle of fish when compared to Dublin, not better, not worse, but higher up the corporate scale. My title improved- Group Product Manager-, my money improved to £5000, my cachet improved. However, I was never quite sure what that meant; my status definitely improved within my family, especially with my doting mother. Unlike Dublin, an important part of the day seemed to centre around lunch at any one of the several restaurants within ten minutes by foot or twenty by cab.

I had enjoyed becoming and being a Marketing man greatly, but the Agency world attracted me magnetically, and after five years, in 1971, I became an Adman and remained one for

Forty years. Up several ladders, often down again in due course as is always likely in this environment. Still, then, you could always be certain that however an unwished 'down' might seem, an 'up' was usually just around the corner.

Two things marked London Ad Agencies – firstly, they tended to be full of very bright people with quick minds and creative brains. At the time, they were probably the best in the world- they worked hardest, produced the best ads, and, as a bonus, they had the prettiest girls. Finally, collectively, they were the best fun and generated by far the most laughs.

They were generous with their time, whether it be for long productive meetings, giggly lunches, or for Friday-evening chatty sessions and, secondly, a reminder perhaps of MBC Worcester Netball players; London Ad Agency girls tended to be very good-looking and worldly-wise and liable to want to look after their clients, both professionally and socially. My early months back in London, still single, quite well off, with frequent access to the Agency world, occupied as it was by very attractive people, made me very happy. I was just getting onto the ladder that I really wanted to be on.

I have to admit before I married, I often found only disappointment when once or twice or even thrice I tried to press my suit late on a Friday evening- only to experience yet another near miss or three!

I do remember my mother's reaction when I told her that I was joining the advertising world- "Do be careful!" she warned me. "Linda says – advertising was all sex and booze and she should know." I was very pleased to find out that Linda (and now, of course, my mother) were absolutely right.

People, including my mother, my brothers, and old and new friends, would quiz me on the difference between working in Production for a Client, working in Marketing for a different sort of Client, or now working in Advertising for an Agency.

The answer was simple – I was, in fact, asked this very question at what was meant to be a final interview by the very dull American Head of an Agency network. I replied at once and truthfully: "Laughter. There is far more fun going on in a confident ad agency than in any Client office in the world". Surprisingly, I did get the job- it turned out to be a bad decision by everybody, but my pay-off when I 'left' in 1989 led directly and quickly to the ownership of our villa in Menorca.

Chapter 9.

Beginning to become a bona fide Madman

1971 - This was the first year I was able truthfully to call myself an Adman. I took to it like the proverbial duck and the water. I also began to travel for both business and pleasure.

I took the 'Nearly' failures at the end of my time at Pond's as a signal to move on, so I did what I had always planned to do. I moved full-time into the advertising world as an Account Supervisor at Grey Advertising, working on Ariel, the brand with the biggest budget in the UK. Though I say it myself, I did the job well. Well, enough to feel confident enough to answer a

Recruitment ad for the Board Account Director on one of the most career-building accounts in the ad world: British Airways. I failed to get the BA job "because of my lack of experience on a truly creative account."- when I think of the very famous television ads- "Manhattan" and "The Face,"- I could not really argue, but it had seemed so so close- another 'nearly one.' One of the most glamorous accounts in the country – British Airways and I failed to get the job!

My responsibilities at Grey were extended to include managing the very high-end Revlon account for the whole of Europe and then Asia: woman-focused, glamorous, of course, but man-run- Charles Revson and, I hoped me. I wanted to run the Revlon advertising account worldwide, but it became another near miss when the US Client thwarted me by decreeing that it had to be run from New York and it had to be run by an American. In a somewhat contrary move, when the Chief Executive of Revlon UK retired, he offered me his job, but I was already on the move and turned it down- nearly right or merely wrong?

I had reached 'home'. I started working life with Metal Box on 29th August 1960, moved into Marketing with Pond's in 1966, and joined

Grey Advertising, I think, on Monday 30th August 1971, eleven years later, I was flying and loving it.

1971 was significant for another more personal reason. I had been a heavy smoker, but in January 1971, I smoked my last cigarette following the publication of the first devastating reports on the effects of tobacco.

Chapter 10.

Being Bright and beautiful

The top of the ladder- your own name over the door? Certainly, a summit but not the very top and not for long but a great experience and, on the whole, an enjoyable one.

After Grey with Ariel and Revlon, Europe, I took a very deep breath and, with three friends, set up Bright and Partners, our own Agency based in a charming mews house in London's cool West End.

We made a memorable entry to the mews; we needed a decent-sized boardroom table, so we had one made, big and very handsome, perfect for our first-floor boardroom. We were about to make our first New Business 'pitch'- for the meaty Irish Distillers account- the new table was to be delivered that morning and used that afternoon. The table arrived on time and was off-loaded, taken into our office, and up a rather narrow stairway to the board room. Well nearly to the Boardroom, but it was too big and stuck seemingly unmovably on the narrow stairs forbidding access to the room and the planned meeting due to start in about two hours. Forgivable but unhelpful panic. A local carpenter came swiftly to the rescue. He sawed one leg off the table, which, with very deft handling, allowed us to lever the table up the final stairs and into the Boardroom, where the starring carpenter glued the leg back onto to brand-new table. He advised us not to lean on that corner that day. I spent the inaugural meeting leaning forward, my arms and shoulders in permanent hover two or so inches above the work surface.

All went well, but we did not get the business – "Best craic of all the Agencies, but you are too new to be awarded our account." Damn it!

Our main Client Was Crown Paints, which was very important financially and good for our Agency because they needed a lot of creative output from us. They, or rather the Marketing Director with whom I had worked at Pond's, made an interesting fee proposal. When discussing money with me - I made a sensible, acceptable monthly fee proposal - he immediately doubled it. He turned to his Marketing team: "By doing this, they (the Agency) will be encouraged to produce their best work for us. It will be excellent value for money".

He was absolutely right and we performed as he predicted.

Our brush with fame came from our becoming the first ad agency to be formally appointed by the Labour Party of which, the Creative Director, and I were staunch Party members. Our time working with the Labour spanned the 1983 General Election under the leadership of Michael Foot, a very fine man but an unpromising political leader. Working with them was a mixture of nightmare interparty squabbles and being able to work with some very smart men (not too many women around!) – we had frequent contact with John Smith, Neil Kinnock, Denis Healey, and Footie himself and, perhaps surprisingly, Arthur Scargill, who fought our corner frequently and lucidly – "We hired experts, let's listen to their expertise."

Arthur was sadly not present at the next meeting, due to be our last, as we presented the creative idea for Labor for the General Election. Numbers were cut down to Footie, Jill Craigie (his film Director's wife), Nick Grant (Labor Communications Director- a really good man), my Creative Director, and me. The proposed advertising- newspapers and posters, radio, and Party-Political broadcasts were spread-out all-over Footie's office floor except what was played out on tape. Disraeli, the Foot's dog, joined the meeting.

Michael suggested that "Dizzy" should help judge the work and so sniffily he did. This was the "Think Positive" campaign that Labor ran for the 1983 election, which, sadly, they lost very comfortably.

I became something of a star during this election mostly because the Party had never had an adman before. This culminated in my being interviewed firstly by Matthew Parish, then a famous British journalist with a UK Sunday morning audience of 35 million, and then a Monday evening interview with the famous American broadcaster Walter Cronkite with a global audience of 145 million, a thorough briefing. The session was slightly tarnished by Mr. Cronkite's inability to call me by my correct name- I was Jimmy throughout, but this did not seem to affect the result.

Our Client List was quite small but good: after Crown, we had Polycell (both owned by Reed International), a High Street presence with Alfred Marks, an Ipswich drink Client- Tolly Cobbold (who turned our cellar into a small pub, exceedingly popular with West End admen) and, of course, we had the Labor Party (its first ever Agency) -one of the most involving. And different Client/Agency relationships any of us had ever had.

Not all the memories were, of course, happy. To this day, many years on, the deaths of Terry Fry and Rob Britton, originally top team players, remain very sad thoughts. The failure of our work for The Labour Party during 1983 to achieve positive results was disappointing but not surprising, and I remain a committed member of the Labour Party. It was our New Business record that was even more disappointing, and in the end, it was this that did us down.

The fact that we had very happy memories from our Bright and Partners days was proven when we held a Reunion party forty years after our founding. Attendance of past employees was very high, not total but really moving.

Lots of near misses, almost all related to too many unsuccessful New Business pitches, meant we struggled financially, and in the end, we very sadly called it a day and sold our Agency.

The Agency had only lasted for three years, but we took it right up the London ladder. Indeed, we nearly took it into the top bracket before I selfishly decided that I would benefit from a significant change, so I handed in my notice in a way to myself.

We sold the Agency and finished debt-free. We had an immense closing-down party and went our separate ways, but we remain the very best of friends to this day.

We all suffered an unfulfilling year running the Agency that had bought us, and then I spent a fast-flowing three or so years as Managing Director of one of the bigger Agencies. It was nearly a good job. It paid well thanks to an impressive Client list, but was staffed by rather dull people, all regarded as being safe pairs of hands rather than daringly or, perish the thought, creatively risky.

I gave my notice to myself again and set up on my own working as an international advertising consultant, in itself a very uncommon thing; perhaps I might even have been the only one. I was only 46 and certainly still needed to work. I had three houses, three daughters (at fee-paying schools), one wife (Emma), two dogs, and five cats. I found I needed to work even harder than I had suspected, so I did. I had thought I would work from home, but I realized this just did not suit me and the way I liked to work, so I rented an office, ironically part of what had been the Paxton offices, full of not just advertising memories.

This consultancy job was, on the whole, a great success covering as it did the last years of my working life, which became full of hits with very few near misses. I retired in 2011 when I was 69 and no longer felt I needed to work. All my work was related to Advertising, and the vast majority of it was to teaching: I created and ran scores of Training programs all over the world. One reason that I enjoyed this time so very much was the issue that had worried me when I started work in 1960 - that I had visited only one foreign country –Holland, and that first trip was to play cricket, not to work. As I grew older, I was regularly and enjoyably on the move. I became a traveller: not only did I earn a lot, but I built a bank-load of Air Miles. I would do it all again.

At this time, the guy who had been Head Boy during my last year at school when I had been House Captain and a Prefect and, I imagine, the same guy who seemed to have vetoed my becoming a Senior Prefect as I, much too my disappointment, had been the only House Captain not to be elevated to the more senior role, a fact that still rankles sixty-five years on, another early example of 'nearlyism.' This guy called for a Prefect's Reunion and almost all those who practiced their praetorial skills in 1960 assembled in a Belgravian pub with their peers 50 years on, many of whom had not met each other during that time. Indeed, it was easy to see why after a couple of dull hours because the Head Boy made a very ordinary speech, which suggested he was still the Head Boy or thought he was, while I was still at best only nearly a senior player. But at least there was no caning.

Chapter 11.

Becoming a traveller

I did not really qualify as a traveller until the very end of my working life when I very nearly overdosed. There are still many countries I want to visit and scores that I want to go to again.

One of the things I had longed for as a boy and a young man was to travel. I did not make my first trip abroad until I was eighteen, whereas my grandchildren, aged 11 and nearly 1, have already had trips to the USA, to Australia, and to much of Europe.

My first trip in 1960 was great from a cricket point of view, if not fascinating travel. When I went to Holland on this tour, I had genuine success at last on the field (most wickets) and also socially (a Dutch girl-Anneke, very pretty but no sex).

My second trip the following summer was to Switzerland, walking with my mother, and my third turned out to be of huge future significance; it was a family holiday on the island of Menorca, Spain. We thought it was so good that not much later after I had been fired and compensated (£57000!) we bought a villa there, which we still own and visit very frequently. After that, I travelled out of the UK at least once a year on holiday, often more, and from about 1966, I travelled abroad for work purposes very frequently indeed.

By the time I retired, I had twenty-six clients scattered around the world, and I had visited sixty-three countries, forty-eight on business and a further fifteen for pleasure. After the slow, late start as a traveller, this may all seem both unbelievable and unlikely.

Well, "Yes and No, Mr. Pither!"

Work and travel have, of course, always been a mixed blessing. Good times have been many and very worthwhile, but there have been many, many 'nearly' times when plans or activities have been ruined or nearly so. I have earned very well, but I have also been ill in Australia,

Spain, Argentina, Mexico, Scotland, Ireland, Thailand, London, the USA, and in France. British Airways notably mislaid my luggage, which always included my very precious course material, frequently, ten times in one year (they sent a case of champagne in compensation). I have several times found myself with the wrong currency, and I lost my money, my passport, and almost my wife in Turkey, a 'nearly' disaster.

Our dog ate another passport in Menorca. On a separate visit in 1999 to Turkey, I lost (left behind in London) the videotape, which was absolutely central to my teaching program. In Argentina the same tape was unplayable as the Client provided the wrong equipment. This was in the days before everything was sent over the internet.

I was paid in cash, a lot of it, after a very lucrative programme in Dubai and then left the 'brown envelope' on the tube when I got back to London – it was nearly a catastrophic disaster, but all was well; it was found and duly handed into Lost Property, quickly identified and returned to me!

These were, on the whole, great years, but there were biggish negative issues. It can become quite lonely working on your own, especially in an otherwise empty office in Piccadilly without a Linda in sight. The travel was on the whole marvellous, a series of very interesting experiences of some amazing places, some beautiful, some, of course, less so. But travel also means absence from home, absence from the family, and the difficulty in selling whatever it is you want to sell, whether it is a Training Program or a Consultancy Project when you are not there to sell it. Face-to-face is always better than the phone or today's gadgetry, and certainly, tends to defeat any lack of contact, which can exacerbate 'nearliness'. Travel does, of course, take you out of sight and mind, but you become aware that you miss possible work opportunities and family occasions simply because you are not near and available but you are able to pay not only your way but other ways as well.

When I have looked back and talked about what has, after a sluggish, slow start, turned out to be a life of much traveling, literally all around the world, I am often asked what have been my favourite destinations and which countries I want to revisit and why. I find it relatively easy to select my "Top 5" and why: Mexico- the gardens in Cuernavaca; Botswana- the animals; Spain- the sun and my house; Italy- the Art; and

Costa Rica – the birds.

I retired from advertising, not from traveling, but from the working world as I knew it in June 2011 after forty years.

Over the years, firstly under the aegis of my mother and usually with the majority of my brothers, we travelled to South Cornwall, not foreign, but certainly travel. (Years later I did the same journey with a family of my own). We did it so often despite the often-awful drive that we became fully accepted, so much so that my mother was invited to pick a Visitor's side every year to play cricket against Gorran, the local side, and so much more so that I played cricket for Gorran and, later for Manaccan with some boast-worthy success. Curiously years later, I found myself playing cricket in Menorca against the island team of entire ex-pats, my last game when I was 60 – 2 for 14 over and out.

Chapter 12.

Being with Great Men

"I will get me into the great men" (Jeremiah, The Bible)

"A long farewell to all my greatness" (Brutus, Julius Caesar). When I retired in 2011, I had a sort of farewell interview with

"Campaign" Magazine in which the journalist, an old friend, asked, "Who are the greatest people you have met in your career?"

I needed time to answer, but in the end, I came up with four different men, men who greatly influenced me- one was my first boss, one was a client, one was a politician, and the final one was a cricketer. I still hold all of them in huge respect and gratitude and with very deep affection.

Bob Tenant: Bob was an elderly nurseryman from Croydon. He had large premises right in the heart of the busy town where he grew a very wide variety of decorative plants, which he sold to hotels, restaurants, shops, and private homes, and he had a big field in South Croydon very near our house. There were a dozen or so glass houses where his plants started life and where he grew acres of Christmas trees. He also had spare acres for other acres this time for chickens, which he reared and then sold commercially and privately in the form of the birds themselves and their eggs in vast quantities. He had a thriving business.

We knew him very well because, until the great schism, he and his wife, Eve, were members of the same Plymouth Brethren Meeting that my grandfather owned and we all went to.

He gave me my first job, which was, for the most part, cleaning the leaves of rubber plants and their like before they went to decorate the foyer of the Selsdon Park Hotel or similar. This remains, seventy years on, the most boring job I have ever had by a distance. Still, I was there for seven years, mostly during school holidays, earning, I think my memory serves me right, £5 a week.

How was he great? Outstanding kindness and generosity and the best living example of how to be a Christian I have ever met. All his spare time and shed-loads of his cash and lorry-loads of his eggs went to the poor and the needy. He also bothered to teach me to learn eventually how to be a boss. For all her life, Bob's wife, Eve, suffered from tintinnabulation. She never lost her smile or her hug.

My second boss was Harrods, the department store as they sold themselves to The House of Fraser, and my work was share transference very nearly as boring as rubber-plant leaf cleaning. My third boss was as a Postman with the GPO, East Croydon, each pre-Christmas period, and then my first real job was Metal Box, but at only £9 a week of which £3 a week went to British Rail and 10s to my mother.

Thanks, guys.

Kameel Shabb: undoubtedly my favourite Client of all (except for one Irishman and one Canadian who are co-favourites). Kameel was the General Manager of Canada Dry (Middle-East) based in Lebanon, in his hometown, Beirut. I was his Account Director based in London. We made quite a lot of TV ads for him, most of them animation, very rare in the Middle East and regarded by most Clients (except Kameel) as risky. His ads worked commercial wonders for his business, with tremendous provable results.

Client meetings in Beirut were not a barrel of laughs even then. I remember a mortar bomb going over The Commodore, the famous but now crushed hotel in Beirut where I stayed when I went to visit him. This frightening event happened after I had been ushered from my plane at gunpoint and gone through four impassable barriers between the same plane and the same hotel. Later Kameel and I had to leave a bar near the Commodore when a posse of Syrian soldiers forcefully suggested we should.

I remember Kameel cancelling my plane back to London – "Too Dangerous from Beirut" and then getting me to Kuwait and paying for my flight back to London on Concorde, then in its first week of operations. A fantastic and thrilling experience! We were going to Cyprus that summer for our holiday. I did the recce from Concorde at 56000 feet and we landed at Heathrow some hours before we took off from Kuwait. I also remember telling him later about the birth of Bright and Partners then in its first week with no Clients, none. He at once booked a barely necessary four-film shoot, our first earnings!

Michael Foot: Michael gets one of my "Great Man" votes not for things that he did but for how he did them. He was an extremely kind and friendly man. As far as I can tell, he was thus to everyone. His manner could lead to seeming indecisiveness because he did not wish to hurt people or their feelings. But he was prepared to debate, to listen, to add thought-through views, and to find consensus. When we brought the suggested 1983 campaign to the Shadow Cabinet for their comment and approval, 45 people were sitting around the table, ready to vote (ridiculous!). The vote was probably evenly split; it needed Michael to come down firmly on "Yes" or "No"- not one of his strengths. I suggested that with the Election under a week away, a decision was necessary; otherwise, we would have no advertising at all, no broadcasts, and almost certainly a significantly damaged turn-out. With one raised eyebrow, he gained strong support from strong players- Kinnock, Healey, Smith, Scargill, and me! My wife had a baby daughter that night, the first message of congratulation arrived from Michael, the second from Jill Craigie, his wife Intelligent, articulate, friendly, interested, and interesting. A great man, a lovely man.

Basil D'Oliveira: Basil was a Cape-Coloured South African unable to do what he did best, which was to play cricket in and for his country. He moved to England thanks to practical help from a committed Mancunian journalist, John Kay, John Arlott, and me. The Metal Box Company, Worcester, stepped in to give Basil a job. He worked for me in a clerical position of no great interest but properly paid. He also had some media work from South Africa. He was not particularly good at his work, but it was work, and he was not just good at cricket; he was brilliant. He played a dominant role in Worcester County and English international cricket; he is a truly great man and a world-class all-rounder). When he was not touring, his winter- job working as a clerk for me was always kept open. I remember vividly my tears at his Memorial service in Worcester Cathedral after he died in 2011.

"Nature might stand up and say to all the world, this was a man!"

Chapter 13.

Being in tune

"The best of times, the worst of times" (Dickens," A Tale of Two Cities")

Of course, I had some really good experiences and, of course, one or two awful ones. Of the two really bad ones, the first was in St. Petersburg (great city) for a Russian brewer (awful Client) and the second for ICI in Slough- the first was an Advertising training program, the Russian 'students' interrupted frequently and rudely. I had already been paid, so I was happy to threaten to stop and leave. They quietened down and we got to the end. The second bad one was a "Presentation Skills" course, and this time, the disrupter was the HR lady (called Personnel in those times), who accused me publicly of incompetence. I know I am good on my feet so the criticism did not hurt only irritate again, I had been paid, so I left. My very best course was another Advertising program, this time for Unilever in Cuernavaca, Mexico- the hotel was a wonderful location, the Marketing Director Client was equally wonderful, the audience was charming and very attentive, and I was on top form. I finished, and the wonderful Client invited me to stay on in the lovely hotel for a week, and Unilever would pay. Furthermore, they lent me a car and a driver for the week so I could get to the big, big sites – Teotihuacan and Taxco- all totally brilliant.

Another really great Client was Orkla, a major player in Norway. Another first-class Client, Robert, who ran probably one of the two best Training Centers I have worked in anywhere and ran it very well. His was in Sarpsborg, a town of no particular beauty. Still, the Training Centre had some original Edvard "The Scream" Munch paintings on its walls, and it had been used to debate and agree on the Oslo Agreement in 1993 between Israel and Palestine.

Almost as good a Training Centre was the Jacobs-Suchard Centre over-looking Lake Constance and managed by another Bright, a namesake but not a relative.

Another memorable time was once again for Unilever, an Advertising program held at Delphi in Greece but never completed. A minor earthquake meant no electricity, and a big snowfall meant no 'students.' This was good Course territory- two years or so before, Emma and I had been looking for Course venues and thought about the amphitheatre below the Acropolis, where when we got there, we listened to a wonderful rehearsal of "Aida." Then, later on the same trip, we arrived at Delphi, where, in their amphitheatre, we watched Jules Dassin filming his then-wife, Melina Mercouri, in some dark Greek tragedy.

Chapter 14.

Being a friend

Funny, topsy-turvy times. Big late changes are not necessarily for the good and may not be for long. Loss of a wife, but I have better relationships with my daughters, so not all bad.

Other factors came into play at that time. My wife, Emma, was fit and well; we had married in 1970, so we had completed forty-plus years of wedded bliss, or had we?

About then, she announced that she had met someone else- Hamish, a divorced Estate Agent with a young son, Rory, at the swimming club, and she now wanted to move out of the boat and into his flat. It was clear she was serious, and I felt I could not or should not do anything to prevent it. I wished her well and we remain friends- sort of. I had anyhow news of my own that I had yet to share with her or our three grown-up daughters, their partners, and our four grandchildren, all under ten.

My news is doleful but far from rare. As I have got older - I am eighty now - I have unretired and I am trying to make myself a readable writer. This is proving harder to do than I expected. It is not helped by the fact that with age has come memory loss and physical imbalance. Nevertheless, I think this will not be a nearly shot- we shall all see!

The loss of memory, especially short-term, is in itself not rare, nor are the problems of frequent loss of balance- nine falls in a year! I think, but I do not know that I may have Alzheimer's (or perhaps I have forgotten that I have got it).

I have a close friend, a very close friend- Roland Oliver.

We were at school together for about ten years, and for thirty or so more years, we have been the best of friends and have maintained frequent contact and continue to spend a good deal of time together with our two wives and, less frequently, our children. About eighteen months ago, I became conscious of the fact that we had not seen each other for an age, perhaps more than a year or so, nor heard from him at all for some months, whereas for a long time, we spoke on the phone at least monthly and met three or four times a year.

Then came a killer phone call. This was between me, not Roland, but with Marie, his wife. After some general chat, I commented on the significant falling away of our contact with each other. Her reply was terse, "Alzheimer's. He's got Alzheimer's," and she burst into tears. Then, so did I. She was, in fact, the first person apart from the medical staff to learn that I, too, had just recently learned that I might have contracted Alzheimer's. I confessed that new as I was to the world of dementia, I had by no means mastered the language of the disease so that "contracted Alzheimer's" might be inappropriate language.

Marie invited me for lunch the following week saying that a sharing of our respective stories might be of some comfort to both parties or even help the healing process. I would be welcome, if I so wished, to bring Emma, my separated but still friendly wife, and, in fact, this is what we did.

So, in due course, the four of us met at Oliver's house. Although I was still self-confident enough to believe I could tell my story reasonably comprehensibly and that, when necessary, Emma would be able to fill in any gaps or correct any inaccuracies, I had no idea whether or not Roland could cope, perhaps when it came to it, he would not want to. On the other hand, I was certain Marie would be a tower of strength.

Roland's condition was much further advanced than mine. His relationship with Marie seemed unchanged, but he struggled to be able to recognize me until considerably helped by his wife, and no amount of re-introductory chat by Marie could get Roland to remember Emma at all despite the fact that they had known each other well for years. Our time together was a waste, limping haltingly along until Marie caught my eye, and a tearful Emma and I slipped quietly away, Emma to her new chap. Me to the houseboat we had lived in now for nearly ten years short journey I could just about manage in terms of accurately maintaining my sense of direction.

Chapter 15.

Being at a loss

So much in my life had changed, very little of it for the better. None of the family in which I had grown up were still alive, and my wife of fifty years had moved on. My three children were alive and well, two with children of their own, but none of whom I had much contact with. I was alone on my houseboat except on Boat Race Day when, for about two hours, the boat would be full to overflowing.

My dog, the third Red Setter I have had called "Handsome," is terribly important to my life, but he is clearly below par. I am about to take him to the vet.

Back from the vet. The news is not good, and the prognosis is even worse. I fear the end is in sight for my beloved dog.

He died three days later in my arms and on my bed. I am not sure if this is the worst loss I could experience. I have spent much more time in the last few years with my dog than with my wife or children. My time with my best friends, which used to be very frequent in terms of meetings, phone calls, and other messages, has had three competitors- Handsome the Dog, Brockett the Doctor, and my growing worries about my health.

Chapter 16.

Beginning to become ill

One thing occurred which turned out to be of real benefit in the long run- Marie suggested that I make contact with Dr. Sam Brockett, who was a well-known dementia specialist and now Roland's doctor and who was proving to be not a curer but a carer, a wonderful provider of support, of real value to Roland. She gave me the necessary contact details.

A week or two later, I emailed Dr. Brockett, and another week or so after that, I found myself telling him my story face-to-face. One personal feature I focused on was that right through every aspect of my life; I had been lucky enough to have had a very good memory, which had served me very well indeed, firstly at school and then continuing through my business career. I had also been physically very fit, and rarely, ill in any way. I played a lot of sports, and I rarely had to see a doctor, and I never had to go to a hospital.

However, this now was clearly changing. An important factor contributing to this change has been a series of falls, at least ten of them. A direct result is that I have now been taken to the hospital not just once but a dozen or more times, staying in three or four times as an in-patient while the medical staff tended to my broken ribs (twice) and hematomas (three times). Luckily, perhaps curiously, I have never actually hit my head, but twice, at least, my mind has quite clearly been affected. Recall of what has actually happened is almost always virtually impossible.

One fall is particularly memorable and impossible to understand. I live on a houseboat moored to a pontoon on the tidal part of the Thames, where when the tide is out, the muddy riverbed is not mud but concrete. I fell off the pontoon. I was saved by the local RNLI and found myself an hour or so later in Charing Cross Hospital, where I stayed overnight. Among an array of drugs, I was given Oxynorm, an effective painkiller with, it transpired, one side effect. I slept tolerably well although in a noisy, constantly lit ward, but had a very, very unusual experience, for me, unique and disturbingly weird. Completely out of the blue, I was invited to speak in the Irish Parliament, the Dail in Dublin, a city where I had worked so happily for a couple of years in the 1960s. Two Irish men did the asking –one tall, short ginger hair, smartly suited, who did most of the inviting, the other a good deal smaller, a bit mousy in an undone, unsmart black overcoat, who did not speak. I could, it seemed, choose my own subject, and I was, I think, inclined to accept, but I asked, again, I think, for some time to consider their proposition. I left the hospital the morning very puzzled by my very vivid experience, thinking about it, including wondering how I would be able to contact the two Irish inviters. I was at Earl's Court Station when, to my total amazement, as I went down the escalator, there he was- Mousy still clad in his undone black overcoat. Open-mouthed, I made as if to speak but, too late, he was gone and, I guess, so was my opportunity to address the Irish nation, and lost would be their opportunity to hear what I might have to say.

I told the ward staff about the entire experience, and their initial reaction was one of disbelief and skepticism. Still, the arrival of a believing Consultant swept this away, the immediate withdrawal of Oxynorm from my list of prescribed drugs, and the start of my beginning to fear the worst as far as my mental health was concerned.

I had a couple of minor falls in the next few weeks- one was in the car-park beside the river where my boat is moored-I was shaken but not stirred. The second was in my bedroom, where I badly bruised my back, and then a third in our kitchen, again only suffering some bruising.

But then came a much more serious incident; I was crossing the road outside Hammersmith Tube Station amongst a small group of fellow pedestrians when, halfway across, I fell, I simply fell. I did not trip; I did not get knocked over by anybody, and some form of the vehicle did not hit me; I did not either. pushed nor jostled, I did not faint, I did not bang my head. I was picked up very quickly by two other passers-by and gently ushered to the pavement, where there was a very convenient Council seat where I was deposited. I simply fell, but I fell hard.

I felt very battered and bruised and befuddled or, as my daughter Jessie put it- "Bewitched, bothered, and certainly bewildered."

A taxi to Charing Cross Hospital again. I stayed there for four days while they tended to my body; really, quite minor bruising, but my undamaged head held a very shaken brain. I did not know where I was. Inexplicably I was sure I was being looked after in a ward at Northolt Airport, a place I have never been to. I then believed I had moved to Burgh Heath, some Surrey common land where I had been some forty years earlier and where I had failed to persuade my then lady friend to make love for what would have been a first time, I suspect, for both of us. While still in the hospital, I made, I thought, another trip, a more exotic but brief one, to the island of Menorca, where we still have the house and where I had actually had the first of this round of falls. Like the airport and the health and the island, this was another hallucinatory trip made only in my imagination.

Chapter 17.

Being a Father

Following my stay in the hospital, I still have to go frequently to Outpatients, and on one of these visits, I had something of an experience, an episode. I felt one of the nurses, clearly a very senior one, looked familiar. She looked about the same age as my youngest daughter, Jessie. She was someone aged about 35, quite small, clad in a normal nurse's uniform, and I wondered if they might have been at school together, but now we're probably out of touch.

Jessie was 35 too, but clearly not a nurse; she worked in the advertising industry, and her 'uniform' was a cool T-shirt and Levi's. The ward was very busy and all the nurses seemed to be at constant full speed with never a break. 'My' nurse was continuously flat out, and I felt rather guilty when I asked her, "Do you have a second?" I said she seemed familiar, and I guessed she was in her mid-thirties. What was her name, and where had she gone to school? She was, I found out, 35 (so was Jessie), and she had gone to Godolphin School (so had Jessie), and her name was Alice McAllister. I then said, "You might have known my youngest daughter, Jessie Bright; I think you must be about the same age."

Jessie is, like her father, in advertising. She shares a flat in Brentford with two other girls, all in the Creative world. Alice remembered Jessie from school immediately; they had been good friends at one stage, but they had drifted out of touch when it came to job time. I then remembered this girl as hyperactive, non-stop, bright but not brilliant, and then, I remembered her nickname – "The Demented Ant" and called. her by this name to her immediate amazement, but then what a response: "Mr. Bright- this is fantastic. I have seen your papers, and I know why you are here. It so happens that I am now a reasonably senior, experienced nurse specializing in Dementia cases. May I suggest something somewhat unorthodox but not in any way banned? Why do you not tell Jessie this story, now our story, and invite her to join me at your bedside at my ward round tomorrow morning? She may not accept; after all, we have had no contact for many years, but you can tell her that truthfully, I believe it could be good for you as a patient, for her as a loving, supporting daughter, and of genuine value to me as a professional nurse.

And so, to home- a Scotch and some thinking- about the boat where I now lived on my own. Should I go on living there?

Was this safe? Was it wise? Would I be lonely? Would my daughters ever come and see me, and would they cook?

Would I be bored? What exactly was I going to do for possibly the rest of my life? Would Alzheimer's hurt? Would it actually kill me? Of all these questions, the one that worried me most was boredom - the thought of having little or nothing to do really worried me, and not being a man with any hobbies except for reminiscing, not being a great reader, or being mad about sport, or gardening or films and now with no wife was causing me great concern. I really felt far less of a person. These worries would have been far less significant and far less of a worry if the pace of working life had not stepped up really world-wide but very especially in Europe and, post-Brexit, in the UK. Everything had to be done quicker, everything was far more technical, and everything was changing fast and frequently. I felt diminished, a lesser man.

I was at the end of my working life and beginning to feel less than adequate. Still, my three daughters- Jessie, Sarah, and Charlotte all relatively new to the working world as it is, but already, it seemed to me, seemingly able to handle what the world was throwing at them with coping confidence and to be able to enjoy it. I felt I could and probably should sit back and play the proud father, acting also with confidence and also with enjoyment.

Jessie remembered Alice immediately and well, without hesitation, she agreed to come with me on the morrow. She felt she would very much like to meet Alice again and was willing to come with me to the Hospital for the next day's ward round and try to learn anything that she could do to help me. One practical move of mutual benefit, which she suggested, was for her to move back onto my boat and thus be able to keep an eye on me and tend to some of my needs. Apart from anything else, by moving in, she would not have to pay any rent, and she could see more of her mother now ensconced with Hamish and Rory in a nearby flat.

I had not seen either of my other two girls, Charlotte and Sarah, since I came out of the hospital. Apart from anything else, I was still far from completely fit. I was pretty sure that they naturally would be inclined to support their mother in her new set-up, and they might have little time to spare for me, none during working hours, and little when at play. They anyhow, apart from their jobs in the Media world, they were also both active mothers, both with two children- Charlotte had twin six-year-old boys, Ian and Charlie-, and Sarah had Josie, aged four, and Sam, a two-year-old. I had a reasonable pension, but I felt both the need to work and to earn and thus augment my pension I also very much wanted to do something during my retirement that I would enjoy and which others could like too. I felt a burning desire to write, and I had a few ideas that I thought were promising, but I did not have a clue how to set about doing so. I needed an Agent or a Publisher, but how did I set about doing this? Help!

That night, I found myself embroiled not quite in another hallucination but in a startlingly vivid dream about my returning to advertising. It seemed triumphantly so but finished in complete failure with a very costly denouement. Nearly a very timely success, but as so often in my real life, nearly is 'not quite good enough' and nearly is all too often 'the summary of failure.'

The phone rang again. It was all three girls- Jessie, Charlotte, and Sarah- a noisy, difficult-to-heart joint call but wonderful, a sort of manna from heaven. "Dad, we never see you. It's our fault, and we're sorry. We now know you are ill, and we are even sorry about that. Can we begin to make up for this by having dinner together tonight? How about eight o'clock? We think Langan's, your old stamping ground, to be the perfect place. Full of good memories for you and, what is more, it's now cool again for us. Is that OK? It'll be on us! We'll be six because all three of our men are coming too. We think you have really hardly met them, but we are sure that you'll like them more the more you see each other- they are all really quite high-flying media men, and they think of you as one of the real stars of the past.

The End? No, not quite.

Chapter 18.

Unbecoming

Perhaps not at all. I have just had a phone call. It was Emma. It was a life-changing call!

She said, "We need to speak." I replied that I was ready to do that. In fact, I said we could do that then and there, so we did.

"We want a divorce. Hamish and I want to get married; the sooner, the better from our point of view. There are a couple of points we would like to raise. You may know Hamish and Rory (his swimming son) live in a small flat in Ealing far too tiny for what will be three of us. We would like to buy your share of the boat, and it is in both our names. You also own 50% of each of the flats the girls own.

Hamish is very sure he would get a very good price for the boat. He thinks it would be north of £300000, and he is also sure it would be a quick sale. "I thought to myself that just shows how little Hamish knows about the houseboat market. He was, I knew, very wrong on both points.

I was prepared for what came next: the next point.

"We should also like to come to some agreement about the house in Menorca."

I pointed out that I wholly owned it. She agreed that I had indeed paid for it but she remembered an informal discussion during which it was agreed that the two of us should own 60% and the girls should have 40% split equally between them. She would like to buy me out and then divide the shares out by 25% each for her and each of the three girls. Hamish would not become a shareholder.

I rejected the proposal for the boat. I definitely wanted to spend the London part of the rest of my life on the boat and a lot of the rest of the rest of my time in Menorca. I pointed out that if Hamish's flat was already judged to be too small, the boat would hardly be better. Nor was I prepared to be bought out of Menorca. I had discovered the island and the villa and I had paid for it. I am the current legal owner of the whole property and the plot of land it stands on. I said I would prefer to keep it that way, but I would be reasonably happy for Emma and the girls to have some letting rights, say, three free months of every year.

I told Emma that I was having dinner at Langan's that evening with the girls and their better halves.

Emma thought it would be better not to talk to the girls about the conversation we had just had, and we agreed that she should talk to Hamish and the girls about my "negative reaction to her proposals." Needless to say, she was "disappointed" and "most unhappy" about both. She rang off.

I had a gentle giggle to myself. I reminded myself of my self-review when I was 46. Time, perhaps, to take stock once again, perhaps for the last time.

I was no longer a son. My beloved mother had died at the age of 98. She would have been very cross indeed at what she would have seen as a major affront when she failed to reach 100, but what an inning! Nor was I still a brother- all four of my brothers had died during the last seven years of what are commonly called 'natural causes' or, as my doctor brother put it "all deaths are down to heart-failure!"

So, then, there was one.

I was no longer a husband. I was still a titular father and a grandfather but fairly uninvolved. I was no longer a boss. I was no longer paid, but I had a meaty pension, and I was still well-off. I still had three daughters; they had been fairly distant, but happily, this looked like changing. We had had three houses, but this would now be two- the boat and the villa, which I was prepared to agree on some form of sharing arrangement. I no longer had a car but then I did not need one.

What I do have is a poor memory and poor balance; I am less fit and, I think, overall, a good deal less well. Jessie's planned presence would be a real plus point, at least for a while, but the future did not really hold out much long-term joy.

Chapter 19. Nearly done

"The end is nigh. The real end?"

No, but, appropriately, nearly so- the story of my life: nearly a top dog at school; nearly a university man but diverted elsewhere; a fast riser in Manufacturing, nearly a young boss but not quite; a fluky move to Ireland but an even flukier one into Marketing; and then I missed two promotions up to Marketing Director, very nearly there but not quite. Nearly two or three early marriages, but none of them were meant to be. Nearly the ad man to run the BA Account, but someone else was even nearer. Founded an Agency but not a successful one only nearly so. Nearly became a politician then I saw the lives they lead. I spent nearly all my later life traveling and then nearly all the rest of it in and out of hospital doing increasing little but passing my time reading, sleeping or receiving a diminishing number of visitors and fewer of all these things as each month goes by

It was, I think, the Walrus who declared that "the time had come"

And St. Peter who warned that "The end of all things is at hand"

Coleridge's Ancient Mariner boasted "The game is done. I've won, I've won"

"All is over" thought Robert Browning

"I have fought the good fight" claimed St. Paul "I have finished my course."

Either Anthony or Cleopatra felt "At the last, the best"

While Shakespeare's Henry IV believed: "Time must have a stop"

Wright- "As I carry on reading, I cannot help but think I am nearly done. I have no regrets, no sense of failure, certainly no fear but full of faith.

"The end is nigh and I am for the off.

Printed in Great Britain
by Amazon